Living
by
the
Rules

Living by the Rules

The Contemporary Value of the Ten Commandments

RUBEL SHELLY

20th Century Christian Foundation
2809 Granny White Pike
Nashville, TN 37204

Also by Rubel Shelly

A Book-by-Book Study of the Old Testament
A Book-by-Book Study of the New Testament
Going On To Maturity
Something to Hold Onto
What Christian Living is All About
The Lamb and His Enemies
The (Im)perfect Church
Christians Only

Contents

Preface

"If you had it in your power somehow to abolish one of the Ten Commandments, which one would you choose?" That was the question Dick Clark put to Charlton Heston, Dottie West, Jake LaMotta, Mickey Rooney, Rocky Graziano, and Dick Cavett on an ABC television program in the spring of 1982.

People of our arrogant generation seem to have no reluctance about challenging God's authority over their lives. It is not only media stars who would dare suggest doing away with certain of the Ten Commandments. Most of the rest of us have felt free to challenge any (or all) of them that get in the way of our own self-willed lifestyles.

Murder, rape, theft, and perjury are in the news so often that we are not even shocked by them anymore. Corrupt politicians, dishonest businessmen, and philandering neighbors hardly raise an eyebrow. Pornography is sold at the corner market, drugs are dispensed in school hallways, and TV brings the coarsest of language right into our family rooms.

Even those of us who attend religious services and consider ourselves God-fearing people are not always above a little white lie, an occasional profanity, or "innocent (!) flirtation."

We have turned away from God, closed our ears, and refused to hear. We have created a world that has no significant place for God in its educational programs, scientific pursuits, movies, music, homes, or hearts. What fools we are to separate ourselves from the only hope we have for making life meaningful!

Everyone is talking about the problems facing our generation. Educators, sociologists, and politicians are acknowledging that we have lost all sense of moral direction as a society.

Only one source of dependable direction is available. And we must turn back to that divine source quickly. We must remember God, seek God, hear God, obey God. We must begin *living by the rules* heaven has given in Scripture.

The Ten Commandments shine like a lighthouse to guide us in from the stormy sea of ethical confusion. It will be worth our while to focus close attention on these *rules for right living*.

This book grew out of a series of lessons presented to the Ashwood Church of Christ in Nashville. The demand for the material in permanent, printed form has been urgent and gratifying. Special thanks to Virgil Bradford for reading through the first draft of the manuscript. Amy Jones' excellent work in transcribing most of that draft speeded up its production immensely.

As always, my wife and our three children have followed the project from the start. They have been interested in it, encouraged me when the work became tiresome to either body or mind, and have never complained about the many hours I gave this book which might have been shared with them in a more leisurely context.

Now *Living By The Rules* goes forth to its readership with the prayer that it will help someone understand heaven's will for his or her life and be encouraged to walk in that holy path. If that goal is accomplished for even one person, its production is justified. If it helps *you* live a better life, to God be the glory and the praise.

Rubel Shelly

Chapter One

"Love does no wrong to a neighbor; therefore love is the fulfilling of the law"
(Romans 13:10).

We Need Some Rules

Frightening statistics point to the breakdown of law, moral responsibility, and even conscience in our world. Figures released by the federal government indicate that there is one serious crime committed every two seconds in the United States of America. There is a murder every twenty-three minutes and a rape every six minutes. There is a robbery every fifty-eight seconds, an aggravated assault every forty-eight seconds, and a theft every four seconds.

The rate of increase in violent crime has varied during the past decade, but the trend for the entire decade has been relentlessly upward. A privately funded study of crime in the United States, published under the title *The Figgie Report,* portrays us as a country under siege. A sentence from that report reads: "The fear of crime is slowly paralyzing American society." Police Chief B. K. Johnson of Houston, Texas, was quoted in a *Time* magazine cover story (March 23, 1981, p. 16) as having said: "We have allowed ourselves to degenerate to the point where we're living like animals. We live behind burglar bars and throw a collection of door locks at night and set an alarm and lay down with a loaded shotgun beside the bed and then try to get some rest. It's ridiculous." The chief admitted that he keeps several loaded guns in his own bedroom, so he knows what he's talking about.

We are a nation under siege. We are a people living in fear. In fact, Chief Justice Warren Burger has asked, "Are we not hostages within the borders of our own self-styled, enlightened, civilized country?"

Worse still, perhaps, is the involvement of so many young people in crime and immoral behavior. Teen-aged Americans account for almost a third of all violent crime arrests in the country. It should shock you to learn that in 1980 70 percent of the people arrested for all categories of crime in the United States were twenty-five years old or younger. And the crimes being committed by young people are increasingly random, irrational, and brutal.

The youngsters committing these crimes are not so much the poverty stricken who are stealing to get a few dollars to buy food; they are children from middle-class and upper-middle-class families who are looking for kicks. And they get their kicks by vandalizing property, terrorizing old people, breaking windows, smashing car windshields, streaking paint on autos, or beating and raping women.

What Has Gone Wrong?

What has happened in this "enlightened" world of ours? *Our society has rejected the notion of fixed norms for conduct, and we lack the internal control that comes to people who have a strong sense of right and wrong.* We don't have standards anymore. We've not only broken the old rules, we've gone beyond that to say that nobody has the right to make rules for our generation. Without rules, norms, or standards, *we are moving toward chaos.*

In spite of all the protests which have been made against such a notion, we really do need a *fixed standard* for our lives. We need both goals and limits. We need a strong sense of what is desirable and what is forbidden. We need the security which comes of having some dependable rules for right living.

There is no better starting point for understanding right living – or for calling people to such a standard – than to study the Ten Commandments.

God's Will for Human Lives

People from many different disciplines are calling for something to be done about the character drain going on in the world. It isn't just an American problem. It isn't peculiar to the Western world. It is a worldwide concern that is being discussed in many forums.

A U. S. Army official has said: "The army would like to see every American parent, teacher, and clergyman work to give our children . . . a firm regard for right and an abiding distaste for wrong." A sociologist, discussing the crime problem among teenagers, observed: "They grow up lacking the internal controls needed to stay on course." A lack of clear moral standards is threatening to destroy civilization.

But where do we get the clear moral standards we need? For that matter, what is "right" or "wrong"? What should I teach my children about desirable and undesirable behavior? What should our society write into its laws and hold up as norms for its citizens? When eminent philosophers insist all truth is relative, famous scientists demand we see ourselves as chance products of evolution, and many theologians cannot decide whether or not to speak of God as a personal being, there can be no standard larger than selfishness. "Right for me is what I want!" "Right is what makes me happy!" "Right for me is what gets me something of personal benefit; I'm sorry if somebody else gets hurt in the process, but it's right for me if I want it and am able to get it!" An impossible situation is created when this creed of self-interest governs our notions of what is right and wrong.

We must get back to the Word of God! We need to know the rules for right living. We simply must have a fixed standard by which to measure our deeds. The Bible provides exactly what we need for the moral direction of a human life.

The Bible pinpoints the human dilemma and gives an answer to it. What is the *problem*? Our self-chosen ways usually lead to our destruction. "There is a way which seems right to a man, but its end is the way to death" (Proverbs 14:12). And what is the *solution* to the problem? Right living is found in obeying the commandments of a holy God. "My tongue will sing of thy word, for all thy commandments are right" (Psalm 119:172; cf. 1 John 5:3).

God has not left it to us to decide *what* is right but only *whether* we will choose to walk the path of holiness he has marked for us. God alone is in position to know what is right and wrong. God is the only one who is holy enough, wise enough, and good enough to be able to tell us what is right and wrong. It is his own holiness that serves as the ground of our obligation to live decent lives.

My moral obligations to you do not arise from some sort of social contract we have established with one another. Those obligations grow out of the fact that *you are in the image of God, and*

11

I owe you respect for that reason alone.

Since God is infinitely holy, wise, and just, we can put full confidence in the things he commands. His *holiness* is at the root of our obligation to moral purity. He asks nothing of us that is not already in evidence in his own character and nature. His *wisdom* allows him to avoid the ignorance and shortsightedness that so often lead us into trouble. He gives rules which are appropriate to all people under all circumstances. His *love* assures us that he will not require something of us unless it really is in our best interests and will never deny us anything we are better off having.

I don't resent the rules that I find God giving me in the Bible, *because I know something about God and his workings.* If I were to stumble across the Bible and read some of its rules for the living of a human life, I might not be too impressed. But because I know of the holiness, wisdom, and love of the one who wrote the book and gave the rules, I am going to take the moral commandments of Scripture seriously. I am going to commit myself to them in the confidence that doing so will help make life what it ought to be.

Right living, then, is to walk in God's commandments; breaking those commandments is a form of self-destruction. Although we speak of "breaking" the commands of God, there is probably a better way to look at our actions. We may *challenge* and *defy* God's commands, but we don't really break them. Divine commandments are as fixed and unchanging as the God who gives them. What we wind up *breaking* in our defiance of God is *ourselves.* Let me illustrate my meaning.

Nobody has ever "broken" the rule of gravity. Although we have learned to employ the law of gravity to fly, we have not broken or set aside the law. Just let some foolish soul stand on top of the Empire State Building and try to break the law of gravity by jumping off. He will break something, but it will not be the law of gravity! In the same way, nobody really "breaks" the moral rules of God. We can learn to live within them – happily, comfortably, and successfully – but we will never nullify or cancel those laws. The foolish soul who chooses to "break" the moral laws of God by living sinfully will only succeed in destroying himself.

To break the rules God has established for our lives is to *sin* (1 John 3:4), and the wages of sin is *death* (Romans 6:23).

12

The Giving of the Ten Commandments

Thirty-five hundred years ago, the Lord God delivered the Hebrew people from Egyptian captivity. Around 1450 B.C. (cf. 1 Kings 6:1), under the leadership of the great prophet Moses, a nation of between two and three million souls left Egypt and started what would prove to be a perilous journey to its Promised Land. Approximately three months after that great *exodus,* Moses and the Israelite nation came to Mt. Sinai. According to Exodus 19:1-8, they camped at the base of that mountain for a full year to receive and learn the provisions of the covenant God was making with them. Although this special covenant was for the Jews alone (Exodus 34:27-28), temporary (Jeremiah 31:31-34), and brought to its complete fulfillment in Jesus (Galatians 3:24-25), the fundamental moral principles embodied in it are *eternally relevant.*

The Ten Commandments served as a core statement of the Israelites' duties to both God and man. More than that, however, they identify the basic spiritual and moral framework within which men of all generations are supposed to live. Murder and lying, for example, were wrong before the Ten Commandments were given at Mt. Sinai; they are still wrong today, even though we live under the specific provisions of the New Testament rather than the Old Testament.

There is no more succinct statement of human moral responsibility anywhere than in these ten rules for right living.

A World in Need of Rules

Our society boasts of having liberated itself from the rigid morality of a code such as the Ten Commandments. This "liberation" has turned into a cruel form of slavery! Bewilderment and moral chaos have resulted rather than the joy and peace we were promised. Sigmund Freud told us that if we would only throw off the repressive shackles of the Ten Commandments we could be happy. So we threw away the Bible and defied all the rules. The personal confusion, sexual hang-ups, and emotional collapses that were supposed to be minimized (if not disappear completely) are now in epidemic proportions. Our situation as human beings is significantly worse than it was when Freud proposed the casting off of the Ten Commandments as a cure for what ailed us.

The Chairman of the Department of Psychiatry at the University of Chicago has said: "Our society and this 'openness' have created adjustment problems for the individual. *There are fewer of these problems when a society has widely accepted standards for morals and manners.* Today, we don't have such a situation." People are happier, more secure, and their lives more manageable when they have some fixed norms and standards to appeal to for direction. The person who lacks a fixed point of integration for his or her behavior is going to be frustrated constantly. The emotional and mental state of such an individual can never be stable. Sigmund may be turning over in his grave to hear some of the heirs to his profession saying, "Hey, rules aren't such bad things after all!"

A few years ago, some psychologists conducted an experiment in Georgia involving the Ten Commandments. They taught prisoners at selected penal institutions in that state to adopt a moral code based on the Decalogue. Later testing showed that 80 percent benefitted significantly from the program. Rearrests at the institutions involved dropped from 22.5 percent to only nine percent. The social sciences are alerting us to what the Bible has said all along: people need some rules in order to manage their lives successfully.

Most people refrain from stealing, adultery, murder, or other similar acts not because they fear punishment but because *they believe such things are wrong*. Internal restraints on behavior are far more powerful than external ones. And when internal restraints disappear, the only way to keep even a semblance of order in a society is to resort to police-state tactics. That is a terrible alternative.

We need to restudy, learn, commit to, and exemplify these rules for right living in our troubled world. This need is the justification for the study of the Ten Commandments in this book. The eternal relevance of the Decalogue will become apparent as we study each of the commandments in sequence.

Are We Turning Back From Christ?

As a study such as this one is proposed, I can almost hear the objection of some: "Aren't we forgetting Christ by going back to study these Old Testament statements? Doesn't it smack of exalting the *law* of the old covenant above the *love* of the new?"

That such a question would arise shows how wrong-headed

much of contemporary religious thought has come to be.

For one thing, Jesus' attitude toward the Old Testament demonstrates continuity rather than repudiation. "Think not that I have come to abolish the law and the prophets; I have come not to abolish them but to fulfill them" (Matthew 5:17). The Son of God regarded everything taught in the Old Testament about God and man's fundamental duties to deity as correct. He did not renounce Moses. He did not villify the Ten Commandments. He did not blast away a worthless and unspiritual covenant in order to introduce the world's first high and holy covenant. Where did such ideas ever come from?

Jesus *fulfilled* the Old Testament types and shadows. Then he proceeded to build upon that old-covenant foundation the superstructure of the covenant which was dedicated by the shedding of his own blood. In the course of that work, he acknowledged and approved every moral insight which was contained in the Ten Commandments. We would be foolish to try to understand the ethical demands of the New Testament without grounding our study in the Ten Commandments.

Also, the New Testament stresses the fact that *law* and *love* are anything but antithetical to one another. Jesus said, "If you keep my commandments, you will abide in my love, just as I have kept my Father's commandments and abide in his love" (John 15:10; cf. Romans 13:8-10). Laws have been given from on high only because God loves us. He loves us enough to give us the rules that will keep us walking in a safe and right path that leads to his fellowship; we keep those rules because we love him and desire to please and honor him.

The word *legalism* refers to rule-keeping divorced from love; it reflects the foolish notion that one can earn the right to heaven by keeping the rules in Scripture so perfectly that God will owe him a crown of life. Legalistic religion is repulsive to sensitive humans and hateful to God. But a lot of people throw around the word "legalism" to show their contempt for having to live by any rule or to observe any standard.

Our justification before God is not based on our ability to keep rules of any kind. It is based on the redemptive acts of Christ on our behalf. We are saved by grace through faith (Ephesians 2:8-9). But one who stands justified "in Christ" will seek to honor the Father in the same way Jesus did. He will seek to show his love for the Father by doing his will, and the will of God has been revealed in the giving of rules which govern our behavior. Christ did not ridicule commandments or claim that love freed him from them. One who wears the name of Christ faithfully will have that same attitude toward divine demands on his or her life.

We will come back to the subject of love's relationship to law in Chapter Twelve and explore it in some detail.

Conclusion

A man and his ne'er-do-well son went deep-sea fishing. When they started back toward the shore after dark, the older man was exhausted from the day. So he turned the boat over to his son and lay down to catch a nap on the boat. Before going to sleep, he showed the boy the North Star and told him how to keep the boat on course by navigating with it. No sooner had the father gone to sleep than the son decided to catch forty winks himself. When he woke up, however, he was frightened to discover that the boat had turned out to sea. They were lost, and the boy had no idea of how to reorient himself and get back to land safely.

He rushed over to where his father was sleeping, shook him by the shoulders, and said, "Dad, wake up! You've got to show me another star. We've run clean past that first one you showed me!"

You don't run past the North Star in this hemisphere, although you can lose sight of it and get lost. In the same way, you don't run past the Ten Commandments in charting a course for your moral and spiritual life. You may take your eyes off them and get terribly lost on an uncharted ocean of sin!

In this series of studies, no "new star" for our guidance is going to be identified. There will be an effort made to redirect our attention to the place where it should have been all along. We have been asleep! We have gotten our eyes off the North Star for right living! It is high time that we refocus our attention on the words of the Almighty and chart a life course by them.

Some Things to Think About:
1. What recent evidence (or personal experience) leads you to think that our society needs to be called back to a fixed and high moral code?
2. What is the foundation for all moral responsibility?
3. How does our knowledge of the nature of God reassure us about the rules

for living he has given in Scripture?

4. Relate the historical circumstances in which the Decalogue was delivered to ancient Israel.

5. Since they were originally given to the Jews, why should Christians be concerned about the Ten Commandments?

6. State clearly the relationship between the Old and New Testaments.

7. What have psychologists and other students of human behavior learned about the value of clear and stable rules for living in a society?

8. Respond to the statement: "Jesus did away with the Law of Moses and showed us that law has been done away with altogether for Christians."

9. What is legalism? How does it differ from obedience that comes from faith? (Cf. Romans 1:5; 16:26).

10. Does one's belief in the grace of God makes rules irrelevant and repulsive? Defend your answer.

Chapter Two

"I am the Lord your God, who brought you out of the Land of Egypt, out of the house of bondage. You shall have no other gods before me" (Exodus 20:2-3).

Get Your Priorities Right

The first commandment asserts the claim of God to absolute sovereignty over the lives of his people. Without this fundamental declaration of divine authority over human lives, there would be no basis for any other of the commandments to follow. This is the *first* commandment, then, not only in order of their statement but in order of their internal coherence. It has to do with fixing priorities in human affairs.

The fundamental decision that each of us must make in life can be put into words this way: *What is going to be the most important thing in my life?*

Live for pleasure and carnal satisfaction, and you will burn out and self-destruct. "For he who sows to his own flesh will from the flesh reap corruption" (Galatians 6:8a). Live for selfish ambition, and you will hurt those closest to you and wind up living in miserable isolation. Think of how selfish Lot separated himself from his noble uncle in order to live in the vicinity of wicked Sodom. His ambition caused him to subject himself and his family to a culture that was against everything he had ever held sacred to that point in his life (Genesis 13:5-11; 19:1ff). He wound up losing his wife to death and his daughters to sin.

Live for God, and your life will take on the special qualities of peace and fulfillment that can be experienced only by those close to deity. You will come to be able to "prove what is the will of God, what is good and acceptable and perfect" (Romans 12:2). The other things that you might have been inclined to live for at an earlier time in your life suddenly seem less important; they fade into insignificance, and doing the will of God becomes the driving passion of your existence.

So the first rule of a good life is this: *Get your priorities right.* Put God first in everything. Let things of the kingdom of God have precedence over every other concern. "No one can serve two masters; for either he will hate the one and love the other, or he will be devoted to the one and despise the other. You cannot serve God and mammon," said the Lord Jesus (Matthew 6:24). In the same context with the verse just cited, the Savior added: "But seek first his kingdom and his righteousness, and all these things shall be yours as well" (Matthew 6:33). These two statements from Jesus are simply alternate ways of putting the first commandment into human language.

Paul took up this same theme of life priorities and put it this way: "If then you have been raised with Christ, seek the things that are above, where Christ is, seated at the right hand of God. Set your minds on things that are above, not on things that are on earth. For you have died, and your life is hid with Christ in God" (Colossians 3:1-3).

The other rules of life will frustrate and annoy you until this one has been dealt with successfully.

The First Commandment in Context

Ten generations of Jacob's descendants grew up in Egypt after he settled there in the nineteenth century before Christ's incarnation (1 Chronicles 7:25-27; cf. Acts 7:6). Although the Israelites maintained a degree of loyalty to the Lord, we would be naive to think they were not influenced by Egyptian culture, morals, and religion. Precisely because there had been some negative influences from their surroundings, they needed powerful assurances at the very beginning of the wilderness experience of the power, authority, and supremacy of their deity. They needed a positive assurance that their God – rather than Pharaoh or the other deities of Egypt – was the one, true God who alone deserved the allegiance and devotion of Israel.

The *power* of the God of the Israelites was demonstrated in a series of acts against the false gods of Egypt. The God Moses represented was able to afflict the Egyptians with a series of plagues which their gods were powerless to stop. Like the Greeks and Romans after them, the Egyptians had a "god" for everything.

There was a god of the waters, the soil, the sun, and practically everything else. As the different plagues came against the Egyptians, they were actually blows against the different things they worshipped as divine. For example, when the waters – including the great Nile River – were turned to blood, that was a stroke of divine wrath against the worship of the mighty Nile. When darkness came over the entire land of Egypt – except for the place where the Israelites lived in Goshen – in response to Moses, that was a sign against Ra, the Egyptian god of the sun. Finally, of course, the firstborn of every Egyptian family died. When even Pharaoh's firstborn died, that was a blow against the cult of the Egyptian emperor. Even Pharaoh himself could not turn aside the wrath and power of the God of Moses and the Israelites.

With these demonstrations of his power fresh in their memory, God gave this first commandment to the Israelites at Mt. Sinai: "You shall have no other gods before me" (Exodus 20:3). The true God is sovereign in the lives of his creatures. He alone deserves full and undivided allegiance.

Before tracing out the implications of this first commandment, it is important to notice the *preamble* to the Decalogue in Exodus 20:2. "I am the LORD your God, who brought you out of the land of Egypt, out of the house of bondage." Quite literally, the verse says, "I am YHWH your God . . ." The *covenant name* of the God of Israel, written without vowels in the original Hebrew text of the Old Testament, is called the *tetragrammaton*. We are not sure how the word is to be pronounced.

Pious Jews of later periods were hesitant to pronounce the name of God lest they profane that holy name and take the name of YHWH in vain (cf. Exodus 20:7). When they came to the word in their reading, they substituted the Hebrew word *Adonai* which means "Lord." The English word Jehovah is derived by combining the vowels of *Adonai* with the consonants YHWH; this form is known to have been used by the beginning of the twelfth century A.D. However, a much older pronunciation of the sacred name is known to us through transliterations of the name into Greek in early Christian literature; most contemporary scholars would adopt this older pronunciation and read it as Yahweh.

The King James, Revised Standard, and New International Versions render YHWH by "the LORD" (all capital letters); the American Standard Version uses "Jehovah."

This covenant name of the God of Israel is used for the first time in the text of Scripture in Exodus 3:13-15. When God appeared to Moses at the burning bush to call him to lead the Israelites out of Egypt, the following conversation occurred: "Then Moses said to God, 'If I come to the people of Israel and say to them, "The God of your fathers has sent me to you," and they ask me, "What is his name?" what shall I say to them?' God said to Moses, 'I AM WHO I AM.' And he said, 'Say this to the people of Israel, "I AM has sent me to you."' God also said to Moses, 'Say this to the people of Israel, "The LORD (i.e., YHWH), the God of your fathers, the God of Abraham, the God of Isaac, and the God of Jacob, has sent me to you": this is my name for ever, and thus I am to be remembered throughout all generations.'"

The name YHWH had probably been used before this occasion but never before with this significance. From the time of the beginning of the Lord's redemptive work among the Israelites, he was to be known by this personal name (cf. Exodus 6:2-5).

The name means "I am that I am" or "I will be that I will be." It announces God's unchanging character and faithfulness to his word. He is the one who is always the same. He is what he has always been, and he always will be just that! He is not a fickle God; he is a stable, permanent, self-sufficient, and promise-keeping God. To the Hebrews, the name *Yahweh* came to be a one-word summary of all heaven's dealings with them. It is similar to the way *Jesus* serves as a one-word summary of everything we Christians believe in and that God has done for us by his grace.

Thus, simply because of who he is, God deserves to be enshrined in human hearts and lives. When he brought the Israelites out of bondage by his mighty hand, he began his commandments to them by saying, "Acknowledge me for who I am! Fix the priority in your heart right now that I alone am God, and there is no other who is my rival or who could ever deserve your worship and allegiance!"

The Place of This Commandment for Us

If you understand now what God was asking of the Jews at Mt. Sinai, surely you see the relevance of this same command for us. If you are going to live by the rules, you will have to give God first place in your life and put the things of his kingdom first in your behavior.

It is no less important for Christians to have our priorities right than it was for the ancient Hebrews to fix theirs properly. In fact, every major failure in the church traces to a failure on this point. Why are false doctrines ever taught among us? It is because somebody has not seen the Word of God alone as true and primary and has thought that his own superior knowledge and insight were as good as the commandments of God himself. Someone thought he could improve on the way God had ordered something done. Why does sinful behavior ever get into your life or mine? It is because we get our priorities confused. We get our feelings hurt and decide we have the right to retaliate; we get depressed and decide it will be all right to reach for some forbidden pleasure as a palliative; we forget that God and his will are all that really matter in this world and begin to neglect the Bible, put off prayer, and place the work of Christ's church on the back burner of life.

Several years ago, a friend of mine was going through the horrible experience of an unhappy marriage. The problems could have been resolved, but he allowed himself to become infatuated with a younger woman. She captured his heart, and he began to have an affair with her. Some of us who cared about him tried to talk with him and offered to do what we could to help him save his marriage. Here was his answer in a nutshell: "I've been through so much hurt and pain that I think I'm entitled to this!" He lost sight of the right priorities. *Whenever we put what we want above what we know is right, we have broken the first rule of right living.*

Jesus identified himself with the first commandment. In the course of a controversy with some Jews of his day, he said, "Truly, truly, I say to you, before Abraham was, *I am*" (John 8:58). Remember that the word Yahweh basically means "I am that I am." Jesus is playing on that fact and affirming his identity as deity. There is no question that the people who heard him understood his statement as a claim that he was divine, for "they took up stones to throw at him" (John 8:59). They were ready to stone him for blasphemy.

Jesus of Nazareth is divine, the Son of God. Because of who he is, he both demands and deserves first place in our lives. He is "the same yesterday and today and forever" (Hebrews 13:8). Because of his redemptive work on our behalf, heaven has "highly

23

exalted him and bestowed on him the name which is above every name, that at the name of Jesus every knee should bow, in heaven and on earth and under the earth, and every tongue confess that Jesus Christ is Lord, to the glory of God the Father" (Philippians 2:9-11).

The Lord Jesus will have the allegiance of those who wear his name, and he will not accept a half-hearted allegiance. Paul explained this under the analogy of a man in military service. "No soldier on service gets entangled in civilian pursuits, since his aim is to satisfy the one who enlisted him" (2 Timothy 2:4). When someone is serving in the army, military obligations have full claim on him. He cannot run two or three private businesses while on duty. He is on service to his country, and that service demands his full time and attention. In the same way, those of us who wear the name of Christ are on service for him. Twenty-four hours per day and seven days per week, his concerns must occupy our attention. Someone on service for Christ cannot carry on two or three sideline flirtations with the world. Kingdom business has to come first.

Jesus Christ is first and foremost in our lives, or he is nothing to us! The practical test of Christianity is walking in the light and submitting to the will of the Son of God. "If we walk in the light, as he is in the light, we have fellowship with one another, and the blood of Jesus his Son cleanses us from all sin" (1 John 1:7). "If we sin deliberately after receiving the knowledge of the truth, there no longer remains a sacrifice for sins, but a fearful prospect of judgment, and a fury of fire which will consume the adversaries" (Hebrews 10:26-27).

For a devoted Christian, every aspect of life finds its meaning through Jesus. Just read Ephesians 6:1-9. Why should children obey their parents? The answer of this text is that it is God's will. Why should parents be patient with their children and train them so carefully about right and wrong? That is one of the primary ways parents serve the Lord. Why should slaves and masters (or, in our historical setting, employees and employers) be so considerate of the interests of each other? Both of them have a master in heaven. As Paul looked at the fundamental relationships of human life, he analyzed each one in terms of what it meant to the glory of God. That is how we need to learn to think.

The pious Christian, imitating his Jewish counterpart of generations ago, would do well to repeat the words of the *Shema* frequently: "Hear, O Israel: The Lord our God is one (i.e., the only) Lord; and you shall love the Lord your God with all your heart, and with all your soul, and with all your might" (Deuteronomy 6:4-5).

The Other Gods We Are Tempted to Follow

Jesus quoted the words of the *Shema* about loving God with all our heart, soul, and strength; he called this "the great and first commandment" (Matthew 22:37). Why is this the first rule for living? It puts God where he belongs. It makes him *first* and grants him *absolute sovereignty* over our lives.

If you turn away from God, you will seek out one or more of three other deities who seek human allegiance.

First John 2:16 refers to an unholy trinity of pleasure, possessions, and position. These false gods are worshipped in many different forms, but everything that competes with the true God for first place in our lives comes under one of these three headings.

When *pleasure* becomes your god, work and duty become burdensome. It bothers me that so many people despise the five days of the week they have to work or go to school and live only for weekends when they "get away from it all." Are we such a pleasure-mad people that we hate anything that smacks of work and duty? What starts as a legitimate diversion for an individual can enslave his time, money, and energy so as to become a sin for him. It may be fishing, hunting, playing tennis, playing or coaching baseball, or any number of things that are good within themselves. But when any one of them becomes more important to you than your responsibilities as an adult, a provider, a human being, or a Christian, it has become a god to you.

When *possessions* become your god, money rules your thoughts and ambitions. You begin to neglect spiritual things and find yourself participating in things you would have never believed possible. You find yourself being devious and underhanded, and you begin to shade the truth in order to take unfair advantage in a business deal. What has happened? You have bowed to the idolatry of covetousness (cf. Colossians 3:5). You have dethroned the Almighty God and put the Almighty Dollar in his place.

When *position* becomes your god, you begin taking yourself too seriously. You develop an over-inflated ego and think you are

25

smarter and more important than you really are. Your "rights" become all-important to you, so the notion of humbling yourself to serve someone else or turning the other cheek when insulted becomes repulsive to you.

John summarized all this when he wrote: "Do not love the world or the things in the world. If any one loves the world, love for the Father is not in him. For all that is in the world, the lust of the flesh [i.e., the Pleasure God] and the lust of the eyes [i.e., the Possession God] and the pride of life [i.e., the Position God], is not of the Father but is of the world. And the world passes away, and the lust of it; but he who does the will of God abides for ever" (1 John 2:15-17).

The man or woman who spends a lifetime in pursuit of these idols will lose both them and his or her own soul. But the person who puts God first and does the will of God "abides for ever." The individual whose priorities are right gains and cannot lose.

The false gods of human experience promise things they cannot deliver. Sensuality, wealth, and fame certainly don't guarantee happiness. Just read the life stories of Howard Hughes, Solomon, or Marilyn Monroe. The "unholy trinity" cannot get you out of trouble. Creature pleasures won't chase away depression, money can't buy love, and fame will not make a marriage happy. All these things together will not secure eternal life, fellowship with God, or heaven.

The idols of this life can destroy you, but they cannot save you.

Conclusion

The God of the Bible is a *jealous* God. His jealousy is a moral excellence rather than flaw, because it is the jealousy of a husband who justly desires his wife's exclusive affection. It is not the sort of suspicious and accusing jealousy some husbands display toward their wives but the sort of holy jealousy a man and woman have over each other from love. A good man would be horrified if anyone else were to get any part of the devotion and affection that he alone has the right to receive from his wife.

In the same way, God will have *first place* or *no place* in your life. He will not share your loyalties and affections. If you will not give him the best and purest of your love, he will not take the leftovers.

26

Enthrone the true God in your heart, and keep that priority fixed forever.

Some Things to Think About:

1. Read Matthew 10:37-39. Would these verses serve as a good commentary on the first commandment?

2. How long did the descendants of Jacob live in Egypt? What influences and pressures would have been experienced there which might have altered their spiritual lives?

3. What role did the plagues serve in declaring the supremacy of the God of Israel?

4. What was the covenant name of Israel's God? Explain its significance.

5. What is the Shema Yisrael? What is its place in the practice of the Jewish religion?

6. Identify the "unholy trinity" of 1 John 2:16.

7. What is the special threat of pleasure in our culture?

8. Name some of the things that happen to a person whose desires are dominated by possessions.

9. What is the relationship between position and personal ego?

10. God's jealousy over us is called a "moral excellence" in this chapter. Do you agree?

Keep A Clear Vision of God

I suspect most people regard the second commandment as an anticlimactic rounding off of the first. If the Ten Commandments were being ranked in order of their relevant importance, this one might be placed at the bottom of the list. It might surprise you to learn that there are *more references to this commandment in the remainder of the Bible than to any other of the Decalogue.* This fact alone should indicate something of its significance.

The *first commandment* forbids the worship of any but the one true God. This command was violated when the Hebrew people went after Baal, Molech, or some other idol god. It is violated by us when we are covetous, sensual, or proud.

The *second commandment* warns against the worship of even the true God under some false form or with a distorted vision of his nature. Recall, for example, that when Moses was on Mt. Sinai receiving these commandments, the children of Israel grew restless because he had been away for so long. Perhaps they thought he had died or had been taken up to heaven. At any rate, they began pressing Aaron to make them gods (Exodus 32:1). Moses' brother took gold from the people and melted it down to fashion a golden calf. When he unveiled it to the people, he said, "These are your gods, O Israel, who brought you up out of the land of Egypt!" (Exodus 32:4).

Which of the first two commandments was being violated in the series of events just described? Most would probably say it was the first one about false gods. In fact, it was the *second.* How can we be sure? As soon as Aaron had unveiled the golden calf, the Bible says this happened: "When Aaron saw this, he built an altar before it; and Aaron made proclamation and said, 'Tomorrow shall be a feast to the Lord (i.e., Yahweh)'" (Exodus 32:5). Aaron was not trying to substitute some new god for Yahweh but was attempting to represent the covenant God of Israel in some tangible manner. With Moses gone – perhaps forever – Aaron succumbed to the pressure to try to give the people a visible rallying sign around which they could center their devotions to the Lord.

The problem exemplified to us by the golden calf episode is still very much with us. Carnal minds find it difficult to think of God apart from some sort of visible representation, superstitious relic, or crude totem. Heaven's real attack in this second commandment is against *false mental images* of God, of which metal and stone images are more truly the consequence than the cause.

Thus we state the second rule for holy living in these words: *Keep a clear vision of God.*

Don't drag God down to your level. Don't let yourself believe that the high, holy, and spiritual God who has created you and whose favor you seek can be represented by something made in the likeness of anything you know in this visible world of ours. God's original honor to human beings was to create us in his image; we dishonor him by trying to refashion him in ours.

The challenge of this rule for living is summed up by Jesus in these words: "God is spirit, and those who worship him must worship in spirit and truth" (John 4:24).

The Second Commandment in Context

When people are ignorant of God, they seem driven to try to represent him by an image of some sort. Paul began the book of Romans with an indictment of the pagan world of his day for refusing the knowledge of God and prostituting the knowledge they did have of him into idolatry. He wrote: "Claiming to be wise, they became fools, and exchanged the glory of the immortal God for images resembling mortal man or birds or animals or reptiles" (Romans 1:22-23).

We humans are *incurably religious.* We will have a god! There has never been a culture or civilization found that was without something it called a "god." It may have been some part of nature – maybe the sun, moon, or stars; it may have been a totem or idol carved by their own hands; it may have been some Great Spirit who was regarded as unknown and unknowable. But there has never been a culture where religious devotions were totally absent.

In his speech in the Areopagus at Athens, Paul talked about the phenomenon of humanity's preoccupation with the issue of God. "And [God] made from one every nation of men to live on all the face of the earth, having determined allotted periods and the boundaries of their habitation, that they should seek God, in hope that they might feel after him and find him. Yet he is not far from each one of us, for 'In him we live and move and have our being'; as even some of your poets have said, 'For we are indeed his offspring'" (Acts 17:26-28). Why are we incurably religious? God made us that way! He created us with a thirst for his fellowship; he made us with a spiritual yearning that is intended to serve as a "homing device" to encourage us to seek, find, and enjoy him. As Augustine put it in his *Confessions:* "Thou hast created us for thyself, and our hearts cannot be satisfied until they find rest in thee."

In spite of our natural curiosity about God, we are often unenlightened in our quest for him. Thus it happens that *idolatry* seems to come all too easily. Earlier in Paul's sermon at Athens, he had said: "Men of Athens, I perceive that in every way you are very religious. For as I passed along, and observed the objects of your worship, I found also an altar with this inscription, 'To an unknown god.' What therefore you worship as unknown, this I proclaim to you . . ." (Acts 17:22-23).

We are naturally inclined to religion. We *will* have a deity. If we are not very careful, however, we will make that deity in our own image and get him down to a level where he can be managed and manipulated by us.

There can be no doubt that *superstition* is involved directly in the matter of image-making. An icon or "sacred object" is assigned magical powers and used to ward off evil. It may be a little silver replica of the shrine of Artemis (Acts 19:24) or a golden cross someone wears to which a magical power is attributed. Both are relics of superstition and unworthy of intelligent people.

Don't misunderstand the point here. There is nothing wrong with a fish or cross or some other supposed "Christian symbol" as a piece of jewelry. What *is* wrong is to attribute to it some special power or superstitious belief. In order to get clear on this

31

point, consider the history of the ark of the covenant among the Jews.

At certain times, the Jews were instructed of God to make artistic representations of things which would be used in connection with the tabernacle-temple. Yet those items became dangerous to the children of Israel when they came to be viewed with superstitious awe. In the days of Eli, the Israelites were involved in war with the Philistines. On a particular day when the battle had gone against the Israelites, someone suggested, "Let us bring the ark of the covenant of the Lord here from Shiloh, that he may come among us and save us from the power of our enemies" (1 Samuel 4:3b). They thought the ark had some magical power about it. The legitimate use of the ark in the tabernacle at Shiloh was being lost in favor of their superstitious use of it.

Do you remember the brass serpent the Lord told Moses to erect among the people to save them from the fiery serpents he sent among them at one point in the wilderness? (Numbers 21:4-9). That brass snake was preserved, and it wasn't long until it became a superstitious icon in itself. The Bible tells us that one of the things good King Hezekiah did during his reign (715-686 B.C.) was to destroy it. "He removed the high places, and broke the pillars, and cut down the Asherah. And he broke in pieces the bronze serpent that Moses had made, for until those days the people of Israel had burned incense to it; it was called Nehushtan" (2 Kings 18:4).

Art, jewelry, and the like are not sinful. *But the irrational devotions of superstitious behavior are sinful.* The worship of the one, true God who made heaven and earth always has been and always will be set against such behavior.

There are at least three good reasons that come to mind as to why image-representation of Yahweh was forbidden to the Jews. First, no likeness of God could be adequate. Therefore any would be false and misleading. Second, God cannot be localized or limited to any one place. Third, God wanted their trust to be in him and not in some magical icon.

In fact, when God appeared to Israel at Sinai, he did so without visible form and only by voice. "Then the Lord spoke to you out of the midst of the fire; you heard the sound of words, but saw no form; there was only a voice" (Deuteronomy 4:12). Why did the Lord do it in this way? He wanted the people of Israel to have faith in his *word*. Prone as the Israelites seem to have been to idolatry, what would they have done if there had been any sort of visible form of him in connection with the experience?

The penalty for violating the second commandment was severe. "You shall not bow down to them or serve them; for I the Lord your God am a jealous God, visiting the iniquity of the fathers upon the children to the third and the fourth generation of those who hate me, but showing steadfast love to thousands of those who love me and keep my commandments" (Exodus 20:5-6). Notice that its violation would bring terrible consequences not only upon the individual doing such a thing but upon future generations. How could this be? It is not *guilt* that is imputed from one generation to the next, but the *depravity* and *immorality* that follow such an apostasy do linger for generations.

Wholesale moral degeneration is always preceded by widespread religious apostasy. Experience teaches us this painful lesson. In the time of the prophet Hosea, the nation had turned away from God. Hosea predicted that the daughters of the men who had committed this apostasy would become harlots (Hosea 4:11-14). Spiritual adultery in one generation led to carnal adulteries in the several that followed! Paul developed this same theme in his indictment of the pagan world of his time. "And since they did not see fit to acknowledge God, God gave them up to a base mind and to improper conduct" (Romans 1:28). *Religious apostasy* brings about *moral degeneration;* you can't have one without the other.

The history of the United States of America certainly confirms this principle. A couple of generations ago, wholesale unbelief took over the denominational seminaries and eventually their pulpits. Now it is almost impossible to find anyone in our society who is willing to acknowledge any firm moral guidelines for human conduct. What has happened? Religious apostasy shows itself in immoralities of the succeeding generations.

Christianity and the Second Commandment

Christians should have a clearer view of God than the Hebrews of antiquity possessed and thus should be in less danger of violating this rule for living a holy life before the Lord. We live at a time of later and fuller revelation of the truth than they possessed. Jesus Christ is "the image of the invisible God" (Colossians 1:15).

He has come among us and shown us the Father (cf. John 14:7-10).

To know what God is like and how to conceive of his person and nature, *see Jesus of Nazareth!* Deity was incarnate in him (John 1:14). In the heart, words, and deeds of Jesus, we learn what the divine character is. And when someone sees the beautiful and loving God who came among us in the person of Jesus, why would he or she ever be tempted for an instant to exchange that for some carnal *mis*representation of deity?

But we have not paid attention to the revelation of God in Christ and have continued to follow the path that leads to idolatry and superstition.

Some modern religions are filled with icons, crucifixes, and other images. "But these are not our gods," comes the rejoinder, "only our *aids* in thinking of and approaching God." This is precisely what the second commandment is designed to prohibit! Aaron told the Israelites that the golden calf wasn't *another god;* it was supposed to be a tangible symbol to help the people focus their attention and thoughts on the Lord. Why was that sort of thing horrible among the Jews but justified among us? Both are wrong.

Otherwise intelligent people get caught up in the excitement generated over the Shroud of Turin, a piece of wood that is supposed to have been cut from Noah's ark or the cross of Jesus, or a good luck charm. All of this smacks of the sort of thing which is explicitly forbidden in the second commandment.

The fact that we do not employ icons in worship, believe in the hoaxes foisted on unsuspecting folk in the name of religion, or carry good luck charms may not mean that all is well in relation to this second rule for right living. For the fact remains that many of us have fostered a number of *false mental images* of God.

Some Common Misperceptions of God

Our God is void of passion and slack toward sin. You and I tend to think that sin is not so bad. Know why? We are sinners! We can't condemn sin too soundly, or we will wind up stomping on our own toes. So we learn to blind our eyes to a lot of things we know are not right. It may be an unethical business practice or devious half-truth. Since "everybody does it," we are inclined to tolerate such things in our own lives and in others. We seem to be able to convince ourselves that even God must feel as we do about such things.

Just look at Jesus to see how false an opinion of God that is. God is *never* slack with sin. Twice during his early ministry, the Son of Man made himself a whip and moved through the temple precincts to free animals, dump money, and scatter men (John 2:14-16; Matthew 21:12-13). They were turning that sacred place of worship into a den of thieves, and he was outraged. And do you remember his denunciations of the religious leaders of his time? He called the scribes and Pharisees "hypocrites" (Matthew 23). They thought they knew how to split theological hairs and find loopholes in the commands of God. They thought they could sin and get by with it because of their mock piety. Jesus showed them how wrong they were.

The biblical doctrine of hell testifies to the severity of God toward sin. Paul wrote: "Note then the kindness and the severity of God . . ." (Romans 11:22a). The God we serve is no sentimental old grandfather who smiles down at his rebellious creatures and says everything is all right. God hates sin, and he cannot allow into his fellowship anyone who is impenitent about (thus unforgiven of) his or her personal sins.

Our God is a tyrant and anxious to condemn. As surely as some see God as too soft and too easy with sin, others see him as a cruel and hard-hearted deity.

In the Parable of the Talents, the servant who had been entrusted with one talent came before his master on the day of reckoning and said, "Master, I knew you to be a hard man, reaping where you did not sow, and gathering where you did not winnow; so I was afraid, and I went and hid your talent in the ground. Here you have what is yours" (Matthew 25:24-25). The man had a wrong mental image of his master. He thought he was such a hard man that nobody could please him.

Look for a moment at the compassion of God that was shown through Jesus, and balance that with the rage he showed in cleansing the temple and denouncing the Pharisees and scribes. One of the things that the religious leaders of his day thought so unusual about Jesus was his association with outcasts and sinners. "Now the tax collectors and sinners were all drawing near to hear him. And the Pharisees and the scribes murmured, saying, 'This man receives sinners and eats with them'" (Luke 15:1-2).

Recall the way Jesus treated the woman taken in adultery (John 8:1-11). Why didn't he denounce her sinful deed with the same sort of vivid fury he displayed when denouncing the Pharisees? The answer is clear: *that woman was ashamed, embarrassed, and penitent over what she had done, but the Pharisees were smug and self-confident in their sin.* God is unyieldingly harsh toward and the torments of hell will be very real for any individual who is arrogant, proud, and impenitent – no matter what his sin may be. The compassion of God is without limit to the penitent, contrite, humble sinner. He doesn't want anyone to be lost; he wants everyone to come to repentance and salvation (cf. 2 Peter 3:9).

Our God is an absentee landlord who collects rent on Sundays and cares nothing about what we do during the week. Some Christians in my experience seem to have a view of God that allows them to practice religion after the following order: go to church on Sunday, drop money in the plate, shake hands, go home for a drink, cheat somebody in business on Monday, curse somebody who makes you mad, deliberately foul up a job to get even with an employer who was unfair, snap at the family, flirt with a neighbor, and so on for six days; then back to church on Sunday to appease God for another week. How dare any one of us think that religion and daily life are separate spheres of responsibility!

No wonder the church doesn't set the world on its ear, if this understanding of God is in the hearts of very many Christians. Christianity is a day-by-day, 24-hour-per-day responsibility. "And [Jesus] said to all, 'If any man would come after me, let him deny himself and take up his cross daily and follow me'" (Luke 9:23).

It is a small percentage of the totality of one's religion that involves being in worship assemblies. Yet some want to make those assemblies the entirety of their religion. Surely the predecessors to this spirit were the people denounced by the Old Testament prophets who said, "God hates your assemblies." The Lord hated their convocations, incense, and burnt offerings. Why? Those same people were robbing widows, blaspheming God's name, and being dishonest in their business affairs on the other six days of the week (Isaiah 1:10-17). The Lord did not want the worship of people whose view of him was so despicably low. Neither does he want such worship today.

Our God is responsible for all mankind's misfortunes and tragedies. It frightens me to know how many people hold God responsible for all the bad things of human experience. Children are born blind, people have cancer, or a loved one dies; someone will say, "It is the will of God!" Most of what happens in this world is *not* the will of God, and it is high time we put a stop to the thoughtless things we are accustomed to saying which attribute them to him.

Imagine explaining the death of her grandmother to a three-year-old girl by saying, "God took her away. It was his will." If that little girl grows up hearing that sort of nonsense, puts it all together in her mind, and draws the conclusion "I hate God," why should anyone be surprised? A God who snatches grand-mothers, runs over babies in the street, and causes planes to crash is a mean and hateful God. Nobody could love and adore him.

The will of God for his creatures calls for our happiness on earth and eternal fellowship with him in heaven after this life. He gives good gifts to his people, and he does not blight lives and inflict pointless pain.

While there are many things we do not understand about pain and suffering in human experience, we do know enough to avoid the mistake of assigning it all to the will of God.

Conclusion

The second commandment is not a prohibition of art, sculpture, and painting. Such work was used in both the tabernacle (Exodus 25:31-34) and the temple (1 Kings 6:18,29). Only when such images become objects of worship or have the powers of a divine being attributed to them do they become sinful.

This rule for living is a prohibition of low, inadequate, and unworthy imaginations of God. He wants his people to have a clear and spiritual vision of him. Only then can we know him, love him, and worship him willingly. If you will think for a moment about how sensitive we are about having bad photos or likenesses of ourselves circulated, perhaps you will begin to understand why a holy God would be angered by some of the false physical and mental images we have circulated of him.

Think the matter through very carefully, see the nature of the loving God you serve in the person and work of Jesus of Nazareth, and *keep a clear vision of him.*

Some Things to Think About:

1. Distinguish the second commandment from the first. Which was violated by the golden-calf episode?

2. How do you explain the frequency of idolatry in human history?

3. What relationship is there between idolatry and superstition?

4. What legitimate place does art have in religious devotion? in the everyday lives of believers?

5. Identify some situations in biblical history when art was prostituted into idolatry.

6. Why is image-making so inappropriate for either Judaism or Christianity?

7. In what sense does God punish later generations for the sins of previous ones? Explain Exodus 20:5-6.

8. Why is Jesus Christ the perfect index to the person and nature of deity?

9. Reflect on each of the misperceptions of God suggested in the chapter. What others can you add to the list?

10. Why would God consider it so crucial that his creatures have a clear and precise view of his nature?

Chapter Four

"You shall not take the name of the Lord your God in vain; for the Lord will not hold him guiltless who takes his name in vain" (*Exodus 20:7*).

Be Careful of Holy Things

Every life needs a clearly marked direction. Every life needs some integrating, stabilizing, and fixed points of value clarification to cling to. The Ten Commandments serve to mark out a direction and clarify the values of one who believes in the Holy God of Scripture. *They are the rules for right living.*

One of the rules a believer observes in his life is this: Be careful of sacred things. This general rule is expressed with particular reference to the Lord's name in the third commandment of the Decalogue.

The very name of Israel's God (i.e., Yahweh) is sacred. "He sent redemption to his people; he has commanded his covenant for ever. Holy and terrible [reverend, ASV] is his name!" (Psalm 111:9). Again, in the book of Nehemiah, when the people who had been captive in Babylon were beginning to filter back into the land and were called to acknowledge loyalty to their God and their covenant with him, here was one of the things urged upon them in holy assembly: "Stand up and bless the Lord your God from everlasting to everlasting. Blessed be thy glorious name which is exalted above all blessing and praise" (Nehemiah 9:5). We still echo the words of Psalm 8:1 in many of our prayers: "O Lord, our Lord, how majestic is thy name in all the earth!"

The third commandment came to be interpreted so narrowly among the Jewish people that they began to avoid pronouncing the divine name altogether. Their fear of some vain use of the covenant name evolved to the point that it was pronounced only once a year by the high priest on the Day of Atonement. At other occasions which called for the use of the deity's name, even when reading from the biblical text itself, they would not attempt to pronounce the holy name *Yahweh* but would substitute the Hebrew word *Adonai* (i.e., Lord) or *Elohim* (i.e., God).

It was not correct versus incorrect pronunciation of the tetragrammaton that heaven was concerned to protect in this command so much as the sacredness of holy things in general. In our study of this principle of righteousness, we shall be concerned to understand it in its fuller and more meaningful sense.

What's In a Name?

We are sometimes too flippant and careless with words. Thus we hear people say, "Oh, there's nothing in a name."

To be sure, a word does derive its meaning through convention and assignment. The four-legged creature we call a *dog* could have been labelled a "pfluft," and the vehicle of conveyance we call an *automobile* could have been named a "quantze." But once a term has come to have a generally accepted meaning within a language, its use henceforth does mean something. For example, you don't want to be called by any of the following terms: idiot, traitor, liar, or thief. And you certainly wouldn't consider naming your child Judas or Benedict Arnold.

In Scripture the significance of one's name is even greater than in our customary usage. It is no mere assigned label. It stands for the person, reveals his character, and identifies his role. This is why a number of important figures in Scripture are given new names at crucial points in their lives. Recall the father of the Hebrew nation as a case in point. The Lord appeared to him and said, "No longer shall your name be Abram [i.e., exalted Father], but your name shall be Abraham [i.e., father of a multitude]; for I have made you the father of a multitude of nations" (Genesis 17:5; cf. 17:15). The man's name was changed to signify the new role he would play in the unfolding of the work of God among men.

When the time came for the birth of Christ to the virgin Mary, the angel told Joseph the miraculous nature of her pregnancy and said, "She will bear a son, and you shall call his name Jesus [i.e., savior], for he will save his people from their sins" (Matthew 1:21). The name was not accidental but was chosen to signify the position this child would occupy in the divine scheme of things.

His name is so special, so *sacred,* that Peter could say, "And there is salvation in no one else, for there is no other name under heaven given among men by which we must be saved" (Acts 4:12).

The covenant name of Israel's God (i.e., Yahweh) proclaimed him as the one true God whose saving power and faithfulness to his people were genuine. That is why his name was not to be trifled with or treated contemptuously. There *is* something in *that* name! The name is not a "magic word," but it is a *sacred and holy word*. It was holy to Israel because it signified the special relationship he had with those people under the Mosaic covenant.

In context, then, the third commandment is not designed to say anything about the extra care one should take in pronouncing the divine name. *It forbids any use of the name of deity that falls short of divine reality and truthfulness*. The name of the faithful and true God is to be used only in such ways as reflect his own qualities. To use Yahweh's name *in vain* is, in the most literal sense of the term, to use it "for unreality" or "in emptiness." The command is surely designed to prohibit false swearing by the Lord's name. It also covers any other disrespectful, profane, or irreverent use of holy names or holy things.

Divine names, institutions, and ordinances must be treated with respect. It is a part of living by the rules of heaven to observe this principle. There *is* something in a name, then, and a generation which prides itself on its irreverence should sit up and take notice of that fact.

Things Forbidden By This Commandment

This commandment *prohibits false oaths in the name of the Lord*. From a passage such as Leviticus 19:12, it appears that this was the fundamental thrust of this rule. "And you shall not swear by my name falsely, and so profane the name of your God: I am the Lord." It is as if God were saying: "Don't you ever use my name in any vain oath! Don't you ever certify truthfulness or make a promise on the basis of my name – 'As surely as God lives, I will do this or that' – and then fail to fulfill that promise! My name is too holy to be attached to anything empty or unreal."

It is not improper to use the divine name in taking certain oaths, particularly those of a religious or judicial nature. The Bible says:

41

"Men indeed swear by a greater than themselves, and in all their disputes an oath is final for confirmation" (Hebrews 6:16).

Many have misunderstood Christ's statement about oath-taking in the Sermon on the Mount (Matthew 5:33-37). He was prohibiting the sort of unnecessary and careless use of God's name which had become common among the Jews of his day. It is wrong to invoke the name of God to certify some trivial matter. Suppose someone says, "I'll be at your house for dinner Thursday night at seven, by heaven!" That is wrong. You don't call heaven to witness about a dinner engagement; you don't invoke the Creator as your certification for something so trivial.

The Lord's words should *not* be misinterpreted to say that one can never use the name of God in a solemn oath. How can we be sure? For one thing, Jesus himself swore by the name of God when he was on trial for his life. "And the high priest said to him, 'I adjure you [i.e., put you under penalty of perjury] by the living God, tell us if you are the Christ, the Son of God'" (Matthew 26:63). The Lord's response to Caiaphas was not "I cannot respond to your question if the name of God is to be invoked!" but "Yes, it is as you say" (Matthew 26:64 NIV; note: "Thou hast said" of ASV or "You have said so" of RSV is an attempt to render literally a Semitic idiom which means "It is so." The NIV brings out the force of Jesus' response with clarity.)

There are numerous cases in the New Testament where Paul calls God to witness that some statement of his is true. "In what I am writing to you, before God, I do not lie!" (Galatians 1:20; cf. 2 Corinthians 1:23; Philippians 1:8). It is not wrong to use the name of God for the purpose of taking an oath that is legitimate, solemn, and proper – a religious oath, an oath in court, etc. But it is wrong to use the name of God in trivial and trifling things, where to invoke his name is disrespectful.

Jesus' point in Matthew 5:33ff was intended as a rebuke to the Pharisees of his day. Their word had become meaningless. Any oath sworn by a sacred object which did not mention God explicitly was considered breakable. His point was to the effect that God is everywhere, and all promises are in his presence and involve him.

Promises are sacred things, and they are not to be broken. For believers, our word is *always* our bond. How much better a world this would be, if people understood this. Husbands and wives need to understand that their promise to keep themselves to each other alone until death is a sacred oath. In most instances, that promise is made in the context of pledging "before God and these witnesses" to be faithful to each other. Does that mean nothing? Children need to understand that their statements to their parents about where they are going, the people they will be with, and what they will do are meaningful commitments – not just a means to keep parents off their backs until they are out of their sight. God is everywhere. He hears all our promises and is involved in their execution. It dishonors God to treat our word with the sort of disrespect we exhibit at times.

"When you vow a vow to God, do not delay paying it; for he has no pleasure in fools. Pay what you vow" (Ecclesiastes 5:4). Have you any unfulfilled vows to God? Have you any to some fellow human being? Give your word cautiously, seriously, and reliably; it is a sacred matter.

The third commandment also *forbids personal irreverence toward God*. There is a phenomenon we all witness in human affairs which defies explanation. When weighed down with grief, disappointment, or bitterness, some people actually blame God for their fate and curse him. It seems to be a knee-jerk response for many. Job's bitter wife urged her husband, "Curse God, and die" (Job 2:9). To his everlasting credit, Job – though confused himself and unaware of why such horrible things had happened to him – did not level an irreverent blast at his Creator. "In all this Job did not sin or charge God with wrong" (Job 1:22; cf. 2:10).

Since the divine name stands for God himself and is therefore sacred, we dare not blaspheme it.

Again, this rule *prohibits the use of God's holy name to voice our unholy feelings*. Shock and grief often vent themselves by means of a profane use of sacred names. Someone hears horrifying news and cries, "My God!" Someone else arrives on the scene of a bad accident and says, "Oh, Christ, what happened here!" Whatever else may be appropriate to say in these situations, to use some holy name as an exclamation is *not* appropriate.

Anger will cause some people to use God's name to invoke an evil curse on another person. The offended person utters a vile prayer that asks God to damn someone who is made in God's own image and a neighbor to the one speaking. What could be more shameful?

How much an expert in language use does one need to be to recognize that a euphemism such as "Jeez!" is a sliced-off form of the holy name of the Son of God? The exclamation "Gah!" needs only the *d*-sound added at its end to finish off the word it is designed to approximate. There are several euphemistic terms that are derived from the word God – gosh, golly, gol-darn, etc. They are softened, toned-down, euphemistic ways of using the holy name of God.

What sort of wicked thinking has led us to think there is a point to profanity? Why do we need words that approximate the world's gross use of God's name as an oath in our vocabularies? The divine name is sacred, and we sin by treating it offensively or by using it to vent our frustrations and anger.

Hypocrisy is another thing condemned by the third commandment. When one takes the name of Christ upon himself to denote a saving relationship with deity, he or she dishonors that name by worldly and unspiritual living. That is hypocrisy.

We are in danger of this horrible sin if we sing "Blest be the tie that binds our hearts in Christian love" and then gossip, "Have thine own way, Lord" and then go our own self-willed ways, or "Take time to be holy" and never read our Bibles and pray. Saying one thing and doing something else is a fundamental expression of hypocritical character.

The Lord's most scathing rebukes were directed at hypocrites. "Woe to you, scribes and Pharisees, hypocrites! for you tithe mint and dill and cummin, and have neglected the weightier matters of the law, justice and mercy and faith; these you ought to have done, without neglecting the others. You blind guides, straining out a gnat and swallowing a camel! . . . Woe to you, scribes and Pharisees, hypocrites! for you are like whitewashed tombs, which outwardly appear beautiful, but within they are full of dead men's bones and all uncleanness. So you also outwardly appear righteous to men, but within you are full of hypocrisy and iniquity" (Matthew 23:23-26).

To wear a divine name is a special thing and not to be taken lightly.

Some Proper Uses of the Sacred Name

This third rule to live by is not intended to discourage our use of the name of God. It is rather designed to insure that we use that name in a way consistent with its intrinsic holiness. *Use the Lord's name in your life, but use it properly and reverently.*

Don't use it to make a promise you do not intend to keep. Don't use it to voice your shock or dismay. Don't use it to curse another human being, a flat tire, or a smashed thumb. Don't wear the holy name Christian if you are not going to make a serious attempt to honor the Lord in your daily life.

Do have the name of God on your lips to honor him. Acknowledge him as the giver of every good thing in your life (cf. James 1:17). Let it be a natural thing to speak of him, his goodness, his will. Think and speak in terms of doing everything in your life so as to live consistently with his will for you (cf. James 4:13-14).

Jesus said, "So every one who acknowledges me before men, I also will acknowledge before my father who is in heaven" (Matthew 10:32). Acknowledging Christ begins in the confession unto salvation that one makes with the mouth (cf. Romans 10:10) and continues through every action of a life that glorifies the Savior.

Use the Lord's name in frequent and fervent prayer. Have it on your lips in praise, worship, and adoration. Use his name when talking to somebody who is not a believer or who is a weak brother or sister.

Yes, use the name of God constantly. Don't take this commandment in the way the Jews took it as a prohibition against letting that holy name pass your lips; that is not the point of the command. Let it come from your lips more often than it has in the past, yet always in faith and with reverence.

Conclusion

In countries where Islamic religion is the basis for civil law, the use of the name "Allah" in an irreverent manner is grounds for punishment. Do those people have more respect for the name of a god whose reality we deny than we have for the one true God whom we worship? From the way we treat the sacred name of our God, one might be tempted to think so.

If your mouth has been foul and profane, clean it up. I know some mothers who literally wash out their children's mouths with soap when they say bad words or use God's name improperly. That may be useful; it is a negative reinforcement against the child's use of that word again. But, of course, that doesn't really get to the root of the problem. You have to get your *heart* purged in order to keep your mouth clean. Jesus said, "But what comes out of the mouth proceeds from the heart, and this defiles a man" (Matthew 15:18). You may need to ask the Lord's help to get out of some vocabulary habits you have nurtured.

If you have been careless with your promises and pledges, start treating your word as your bond. It is given in the presence of God always, and your integrity is on the line whenever you speak.

We are not through with our words once they have been spoken. The Lord said we will meet them again in Judgment; we will be justified or condemned on the basis of them. "I tell you, on the day of judgment men will render account for every careless word they utter; for by your words you will be justified, and by your words you will be condemned" (Matthew 12:36-37).

Some Things to Think About:

1. What narrow interpretation did the rabbis place on the third commandment? How did that miss its point?

2. Identify a number of Bible characters whose names were changed. Explain the significance of each.

3. What does it mean to use the name of the Lord "in vain"?

4. Does the Bible prohibit all oath-taking (i.e., swearing) by the name of God? Defend your answer.

5. How is this rule broken by personal irreverence toward God?

6. What is your personal view of cursing? the use of God's name as an exclamation? euphemisms for the divine name?

7. How does the sin of hypocrisy relate to this commandment?

8. Identify some proper and holy uses of the name of God.

9. What is the general attitude of our culture toward the name of God?

10. Reflect on Matthew 12:36-37. Does this text comfort or frighten you?

Chapter Five
"Remember the sabbath day, to keep it holy" (Exodus 20:8).

Use Your Time to God's Glory

The sabbath is a peculiarity of the Jewish religion and one of its most interesting features. Our English word "sabbath" is from a Hebrew term which means cessation or rest. This holy day of rest was observed on Saturday, the seventh day of the week.

The sabbath *recalled God's rest after six days of creative work*. "And on the seventh day God finished his work which he had done, and he rested on the seventh day from all his work which he had done" (Genesis 2:3: cf. Exodus 20:11). Beyond that, it was instituted to allow the Jews *a fixed time for deliberate worship to Yahweh*. The practice of Jesus about sabbath observance was typical of pious Jews of his time: "And he came to Nazareth, where he had been brought up; and he went to the synagogue, as his custom was, on the sabbath day" (Luke 4:16). Furthermore, there was a *humanitarian aspect* to the sabbath law. Deuteronomy 5:14 indicates that a man was to allow his children, servants, animals, and everything under his authority to use that day for rest and refreshment.

There is no evidence that the seventh day was observed as a special day of rest and worship prior to the giving of the Decalogue. As the Hebrew nation under Moses neared Mt. Sinai just prior to the giving of the Law, God's prophet gave the people detailed instruction about gathering extra food, preparing it in advance, and observing a strict day of rest before the Lord (Exodus 16:22-30). This would seem to indicate that the observance was something with which the Jews were unfamiliar. It appears to have been a new religious observance to them here and was bound as

47

a perpetual ordinance at Mt. Sinai.

Although faithful sabbath observance was evidently slow in coming (cf. Nehemiah 13:15-22), by Jesus' day it was kept with a vengeance. By then it had become such a distinctive – even oppressive – feature of the Jewish religion that anyone who knew anything at all about the Jews were aware of their strict refusal to work on the seventh day of the week.

There is good evidence to the effect that this commandment has been more abused than understood throughout history. So abused was it in Hebrew history that the sabbath became a heavy-handed and harsh commandment to the Jews rather than a delight-ful experience. And some have tried to incorporate something of the legalistic view of the sabbath that made it so oppressive to the Jews into the religion of Jesus Christ.

It is worth the effort to study this commandment closely for the sake of a clear perspective of its original intent and significance. Such an understanding will help us learn a badly needed lesson about balance in our hectic and sometimes frustrating world.

Sabbath Observance Under the Law of Moses

Under the Law of Moses, the sabbath was a holy day of rest from common labor and a time for devotion and worship to God. So strict was the enforcement of cessation from labor that the Jews were specifically told that even such things as lighting a new fire were not permitted on the sabbath (Exodus 35:3). The Old Tes-tament tells of a man who violated this rule by gathering sticks on the sabbath; the Lord told Moses to see that he was stoned to death for his infraction of the rule against work on that day (Numbers 15:32-36).

Although the negatives of the day are usually emphasized, we should not overlook the fact that the Law permitted necessary work such as priestly functions, caring for the sick, and saving an animal's life on the sabbath. The Pharisees once accused Jesus of allowing his disciples to break the sabbath by plucking and eating grain as they walked through a field. They said, "Look, your disciples are doing what is not lawful to do on the sabbath" (Matthew 12:2). The Law contains no such prohibition against eating to sustain life. The Lord answered, "Have you not read in the law how on the sabbath the priests in the temple profane the sabbath, and are guiltless?" (Matthew 12:5). Those priests on duty at the temple did not actually "profane the sabbath" by performing their duties on that holy day. Jesus was using the language of *irony* to rebuke the Pharisees. In effect, he was saying, "Look, as you interpret the sabbath regulation, nobody can lift a finger to do anything on that day. By your interpretation, then, even the priests sin whenever they slay a sacrificial animal and place it on the altar on the sabbath. Surely you don't believe that."

Later in the same setting, Jesus asked, "What man of you, if he has one sheep and it falls into a pit on the sabbath, will not lay hold of it and lift it out? Of how much more value is a man than a sheep! So it is lawful to do good on the sabbath" (Matthew 12:11-12). The Savior's point here – one which many still do not appreciate – is to the effect that the original sabbath commandment was something very different than Jewish tradition had made it. It was much gentler and more humane than the Pharisees could appreciate.

The Jewish rabbis had taken a wholesome injunction to such absurd extremes that the sabbath was hateful to many Jews of Jesus' day. A lengthy tractate of the *Mishnah* lists thirty-nine acts forbidden on the sabbath. Among these are such things as carrying something from one place to another, separating two threads, writing as many as two letters of the alphabet, tying a knot, etc. Each of these prohibitions generated debate as to what constituted an offense of its type. Did wearing an artificial limb constitute a violation of the injunction against burden bearing? Some rabbis said it did, but others disagreed.

The same teachers of the Law added precautionary measures intended to prevent acts which might lead to breaking the sabbath. For example, a tailor was not allowed to take his needles home or a scribe his pen on the eve of the sabbath! The Law of Moses was never intended for such a purpose. Jesus tried to put things back in their proper perspective by saying, "The sabbath was made for man, not man for the sabbath" (Mark 2:27).

Jewish legalism made a beautiful event into a harsh and hateful ritual. It made the day a burden and its observance an object of ridicule. From the start, God had intended it to bless rather than burden his people. Families and friends could be together, devotion to God could be shared, and the spirit and body refreshed. How far away from that ideal did the Jews remove themselves!

Some Issues of Doctrine

Before turning to the practical relevance of this fourth rule for living to our present situation, there are several questions of a doctrinal nature which need to be addressed and answered. With the sabbath commandment more than any other, there are some differences between what was required of fleshly Israel under the Law and what is required of spiritual Israel under the new covenant. We need to clarify those matters before going further.

Why do Christians observe Sunday as the day of worship rather than Saturday?

Sometimes it is suggested that the church took the sabbath idea from Judaism and gradually changed its day of worship from the seventh day of the week to the first. A look at the New Testament evidence proves that Sunday has been the special day of worship for Christians from the very beginning (cf. Acts 20:7; 1 Corinthians 16:2). Sunday is sacred as the day on which Christ rose from the dead (Matthew 28:1) and on which the church began (Acts 2:1ff). Early on it came to be known as "the Lord's Day" (Revelation 1:10).

While Sunday did not become a state holiday until Constantine made it such in 321, it has been the special day of Christian worship from the day the church was founded.

Is it correct to refer to Sunday as the "Christian Sabbath?"
No. That terminology is not used in Scripture, and we ought not use it either.

The sabbath is distinctively Jewish. Yahweh told Moses, "Therefore the people of Israel shall keep the sabbath, observing the sabbath throughout their generations, as a perpetual covenant. It is a sign for ever between me and the people of Israel . . ." (Exodus 31:16-17a). Sabbath observance has never been bound on anyone other than the Jews, and it is a contradiction to talk about a "*Christian* sabbath." The sabbath is *Jewish* from beginning to end of its observance in the Bible.

To what degree is our behavior on Sunday to be governed by the sabbath rules?

I once had extensive conversations with a group of men who belonged to a religious sect which held that the behavior of Christians should be regulated strictly by the sabbath rules of the Old Testament. On Sundays these people forbid their children to go out into the yard and play. They will not allow them to toss a

50

football or play on a tire swing, because they feel it is a violation of the sabbath rule. The family cannot pick up a basket of food and walk out under the trees for a picnic, for they think this would violate the rule against carrying burdens on the sabbath. This is a monstrous misapplication of the sabbath rules to our behavior on Sunday.

On the other hand, this is not to say that Christians should treat Sunday as just another business-as-usual day. After all, it is the *Lord's* and should be used accordingly. It should be used in special ways that indicate our devotion to him. It is a day for public worship with the saints. It is a fine time for a busy family to be together and strengthen its ties of communication and love. It is a good day for seeing someone who is sick or spiritually weak. All these are things we may not be able to do on ordinary workdays of the week; they honor the Lord on *his* day of the week.

All the pointless haggling and false teaching done over the sabbath issue trace to a fundamental misunderstanding of what is at stake in this rule for living. The sabbath commandment has no precise equivalent in the New Testament, but the underlying principle holds good for all people at all times in history. We shall spend the remainder of our study in an effort to identify and explain that principle.

Stewards of Time

What is the *principle* embodied in the fourth commandment? It is simply this: *God wants to be honored in the use we make of our time.*

The first three commands call us to honor God by putting him first in our *lives,* sanctifying him in our *hearts,* and honoring him with our *lips;* the fourth calls us to glorify him by our use of precious *time.* All the time we have on earth in a lifetime is God's gift to us and is to be used for his purposes.

Time is the very essence of life, and the Bible contains several emphatic reminders of our obligation to use it wisely. "Look carefully then how you walk, not as unwise men but as wise, making the most of the time, because the days are evil. Therefore do not be foolish, but understand what the will of the Lord is" (Ephesians 5:15-17). "Conduct yourselves wisely toward outsiders, making the most of the time" (Colossians 4:5).

A Psalm attributed to Moses contains this prayer: "So teach us

51

to number our days that we may get a heart of wisdom" (Psalm 90:12). The sentiment here is essentially the same as the one we sing in a familiar hymn: "Take my moments and my days,/ Let them flow in ceaseless praise."

We appear to have done a better job of teaching *stewardship* in relation to talent and money than in relation to time. It is Satan who leads us to misuse and squander time. We defeat him by learning to budget time so as to master it rather than being mastered by it.

Good stewardship of time under the Lord Jesus involves learning to live a well-ordered life which has a place for family, exercise, rest, chores, recreation, wage earning, and sleep as well as for prayer, Bible reading, and church assemblies. We disgrace ourselves and horrify our God by living in a frenzy so as to break both health and sanity! Good religion is, among other things, good sense about the use of precious time.

A great many books are being written about time management. Perhaps it would do you good to read one or two. But read with a particular perspective. Don't read with a view toward the question "What is the best way to use time so as to make money with it?" Read with the question in mind "What is the best way to use time so as to manage my entire life to the glory of God?"

Stewardship of your time under God involves giving priority to your family. Don't let a busy life crowd out your husband, wife, or children. Don't let your family go to pieces simply because you don't have time to get involved with the people you love most in all the world. Families that fail don't set out to destroy each other. Their lives just get so fragmented by the careless use of time that they never have time to get to know each other and therefore can never be of any real help to one another.

Leave some time for exercise and taking care of your health. It is shameful that more hasn't been said in pulpits about the care God wants us to take of our physical bodies. The body of a Christian is a temple of the Holy Spirit (cf. 1 Corinthians 6:19-20), and the way many of us abuse our bodies in a sin. Putting alcohol, tobacco, or other harmful substances into them is wrong. So are overeating, failing to control one's weight, or being so sedentary as to destroy one's health and well-being.

All of life belongs to God! Everything is under the Lordship of Christ for the believer, and everything is done to honor him (cf. 1

Corinthians 10:31).

Balance in Your Life

There is a time for work. "Six days you shall labor, and do all your work" (Exodus 20:9). Some people fail to see that a full work week is envisioned by this rule for good living. The desire to do less and less while receiving more money and leisure for it is a blight on the modern world. It is a character defect within the person who harbors such a desire.

Our best interest is served by work. In the Garden of Eden – *before* the Fall and curse – man was given the responsibility of working. "The Lord God took the man and put him in the garden of Eden to till it and keep it" (Genesis 2:15). Scripture demands honest labor of all who are able to work. Paul wrote: "For even when we were with you, we gave you this command: If anyone will not work, let him not eat" (2 Thessalonians 3:10).

Work is honorable, and no spiritual person resents it or envies the parasite who gets along without it.

There is a time for rest. Though we are meant to work, God did not create our bodies and minds for constant tension and uninterrupted exertion. There has to be a time of backing away for rest and renewal. At the end of the day, at the end of a work week, when some difficult project has been completed, you have to turn loose and let it go.

After you have worked hard and finished your task, don't feel guilty for enjoying a period of rest and relaxation. Rest is as honorable as the honest and hard work that make it sweet. The two go together in God's plan for a good life.

There is a time for worship. Christians worship God in many different settings – both private and public. But Sunday is a time for heightened sensitivity to spiritual concerns. Worship must be primary on the Lord's Day (cf. Hebrews 10:25).

It is not sinful for a Christian to work on Sunday, if his work is of a vital public nature (e.g., medical services, transporation, etc.) or if he is being forced to work on that day in order to hold a job that supports his family. On the other hand, it seems impossible to justify a Christian choosing a work situation which rules out the opportunity of assembling with the saints. There are surely some circumstances where a child of God would feel the need to change jobs in order to be free to fulfill his commitments to the Lord.

Conclusion

The fourth rule God wants his people to live by was never intended to be oppressive. It was designed to be wholesome, encouraging, and positive. God wanted to give us direction for living a balanced life, with place for work, rest, and worship. All three are to the glory of God in a believer's life.

A life with these elements in correct balance is rich and rewarding. Do you have them in balance in yours?

Some Things to Think About:

1. When did the sabbath originate as a day of special worship to Yahweh? Do you find any evidence that it was observed prior to the Mt. Sinai experience?

2. What was the purpose of this commandment? How was it supposed to be observed?

3. How was the regulation about the sabbath being interpreted and enforced at the time of Jesus?

4. What was Jesus' opinion of the prevailing practices of the Jews concerning the sabbath?

5. Define the relationship between the sabbath and the Lord's Day.

6. What is the central principle embodied in this commandment?

7. What are some of the most practical things you have learned that assist you in your personal stewardship of time?

8. What is the general attitude of people toward work and responsibility? Is it a healthy one? Is it Christian?

9. Why does the Lord require rest as well as work in our lives?

10. Decide on some proper and Christ-honoring ways to use Sunday. Do we ever have problems in this regard?

Chapter Six

"Honor your father and your mother, that your days may be long in the land which the Lord your God gives you" (Exodus 20:12).

Honor Your Parents

No one is ever going to improve on the Ten Commandments as a basic statement of man's religious and moral responsibilities. The rules worth living by for a lifetime are more succinctly wrapped up in these ten statements than in any other small package conceivable.

The fifth of these commands brings us to a fundamental responsibility in human relations. The commandment says: "Honor your father and your mother." Our own common sense tells us that we need some rules for preserving and strengthening family life.

The *family* is being challenged for its right to endure. Many are choosing to forego marriage; from 1970 to 1980 the number of people under age twenty-five living alone tripled from 556,000 to 1,670,000. Others are substituting life together without marriage for the traditional marriage relationship; the Census Bureau says over 1,500,000 couples are living together without being married.

Those who do choose the traditional arrangement are having problems keeping things together and achieving stability within their marriages. The divorce rate has increased fifteenfold in the past century and doubled in the past decade. A female member of the Maryland legislature introduced a bill recently to legalize a renewable three-year contract for marriage!

Lives are shattering like eggshells under so many thoughtless feet. Divorce is more traumatic than death. Death has a finality about it that can be accepted, but divorce is never over. For both adults and any children involved, it hangs on to haunt them for

55

the rest of their lives. One million children a year suffer the breakup of their families; one of every five children in the United States today lives with only one of his parents. A study of 18,000 children from one-parent families done by the National Association of Elementary School Principals and the Kettering Foundation reports that such children achieve less in school, are absent more, and have more disciplinary problems. Can we seriously think the problems of such a situation are any fewer or less debilitating for the adults in these homes?

Something that has gotten less attention than the statistics about divorce and the harm done to children by family collapse is the problem of *abused parents* in homes. Annually some eight million children assault their parents. Eighteen out of every one hundred children in the United States will assault one or both of their parents in any given year in this country.

The family is primary to God as a means for blessing and guiding human lives. With the failure of so many homes in the different ways already identified, the will of God is being thwarted too frequently. One of the rules for right living points to the need for keeping the family strong through proper relationships between children and their parents. It deserves our careful study.

Respect for Parents: A Forgotten Virtue

The Old Testament places great emphasis on respect for older persons generally and for parents in particular. "You shall rise up before the hoary head, and honor the face of an old man, and you shall fear your God: I am the Lord" (Leviticus 19:32). "Whoever strikes his father or his mother shall be put to death. . . . Whosoever curses his father or his mother shall be put to death" (Exodus 21:15,17; cf. Deuteronomy 21:18-21).

Other ancient cultures – notably the Chinese – also stressed the same virtue of respect for parents. Older people were given a place of special honor. Parents were afforded a respect that bordered on veneration. Today this tradition has come to be despised. *Age* is abhorred, and *youth* is idolized. Our values in this regard have been turned on their head.

Jesus castigated the Pharisees of his day for making havoc of the fifth commandment. "And he said to them, 'You have a fine way of rejecting the commandment of God, in order to keep your tradition! For Moses said, "Honor your father and your mother"';

and, "He who speaks evil of father or mother, let him surely die"; but you say, "If a man tells his father or his mother, What you would have gained from me is Corban" (that is, given to God) – then you no longer permit him to do anything for his father and mother, thus making void the word of God through your tradition which you hand on'" (Mark 7:9-13).

We don't know the details of this business of pledging one's estate to God in order to be relieved of obligation to one's parents. But in certain circumstances – whether with sinister intent or innocently on the part of the one doing it – an individual could pledge his substance to God. If a later situation of need arose involving his parents, certain legalistic rabbis said it was wrong to use those resources for the benefit of his needy parents. Their tradition was being allowed to cancel out a primary command of God.

Today there are a number of traditions developing in our culture which, though not from a religious source, are causing many people to dishonor their parents. Parents are sometimes shoved away from their children. The children refuse any financial or emotional support to their parents. It isn't wrong to place one's aged father or mother in a nursing home; sometimes that is the best place for the person to get the medical attention he or she needs. But it *is* wrong to dump them there and make them feel unwanted and unloved.

A friend of mine was in the hospital recently and shared a double room with an old man facing serious surgery. The man called his son, who lived in the same town where he was hospitalized, and asked him to come and be with him. The son explained that he was so tied up with his business that he just couldn't spare the time! Of course, I don't know what sort of a relationship that father and son had over the years. Even if it was a horrible one and due to the father's failure, that frightened old man deserved more than he got from his son in that situation.

Paul put this commandment into its Christian context in Ephesians 6:2-3. "'Honor your father and mother' (this is the first commandment with a promise), 'that it may be well with you and that you may live long on the earth.'" In still another epistle he wrote, the same apostle said that disrespect for parents is a sign of apostasy from God (Romans 1:30; cf. 2 Timothy 3:2).

Heaven wants children to respect their parents. Whether it has to do with providing for them financially or doing something so trivial as holding a door or carrying grocery bags, parents have a right to certain courtesies from their children. Those who help build a society where age has a place of honor secure that place for themselves one day; those who abhor their parents and resent the wisdom of age will reap the fruits of their disrespect.

Why Parents Should Be Honored

If anyone should ask for justification of this rule about honoring our parents, at least four things come to mind immediately.

First, parents should be honored because *it is right*. "Children, obey your parents in the Lord, for this is right" (Ephesians 6:1). Even without biblical revelation, there are some things that commend themselves to us as proper and right. Surely one of those things is showing honor to the man and woman responsible for bringing you into the world, feeding you, getting your cavities filled, nursing you when you were sick, and doing the million other things that go with being a parent. Lest anyone miss this obvious truth, Paul has said it in so many words in the Bible. Honor your parents. It's the right thing to do.

God has placed parents in a certain relationship of responsibility to and authority over their children. To resist or show contempt for any God-ordained authority is to resist and dishonor God (cf. Romans 13:1b). What applies to our relationship with government surely has significance for our relationship with our parents. Dishonoring one's parents is an insult to Almighty God.

Second, children owe their parents a *huge debt* for the provision and love received at their hands. Not one of us will ever know the many, many sacrifices our parents made to feed us, send us to school, help us get started with our own families, or become established in business or a profession. Even if they were unable to help with money in those situations, they helped by being the one pair of people in all the world that we knew would always believe in us, love us even when we failed at something, and never kick us while we were down.

Many a man or woman has been a "prodigal child" at one time or other. The incident may have been small, but something happened that embarrassed and discouraged you. The episode made you wonder whether you could ever face the world again or try to recoup your losses. What has saved many of us in those low moments – especially during adolescence – was the knowledge that there was a father and/or mother at home whose love was still warm. As with the original prodigal son of Luke 15:11-32, he got himself estranged from his parents for a few hours, a few days, or maybe even a few years. But when he remembered his father's love and made a move in the direction of home, the father went running to meet and embrace his child. The Parable of the Prodigal Son is such a believable story, for it has been repeated time and time again in history.

How will we ever repay our parents for their time, money, and love? Yet some children neglect and abandon their parents when they are so ill that they must be cared for "as if they were babies." They cared for us when we *were* babies! Is there no shame in turning away from their helplessness? In pre-Social Security days, old people had no one but their children to turn to in times of need; today they still need the loving concern of their children. Having rent, groceries, and utility money is not enough. They need to feel that they are not an imposition in the lives of their children, that they have a place where somebody remembers them, cares about them, and takes time out of a busy life to pay attention to them.

Third, children can always derive *great personal benefit* from seeking and heeding the counsel of their parents. A child who has finished high school or a few years of college may already have more education than his parents; what he may not realize is that he is not yet as smart as his parents. There are some things that nobody learns except by living, having experience, failing at some things and bouncing back. The best lessons about life don't come from college texts. They come from the good counsel of godly parents. If you have a relationship with people who have lived long enough to learn those lessons and who will share their wisdom with you, your life will be blessed. Most likely, those people will be your parents.

Fourth, we should honor our parents because *the day will come when we cannot show them the honor we would like to give.* Some who will read these lines don't have your parents with you any longer. I hope you don't have to look back and say, with regret, "You know, I never told my father how much I loved him. As many times as I was in her house, ate her delicious cooking, and received her unfailing love, I never told my mother how much I loved her." I hope you will be able to tell them in heaven. But why should a mother or father have to wait to hear a child express genuine love?

If you still have your parents but have been reluctant, embarrassed, or simply thoughtless about giving them explicit statements and expressions of your love, don't make the mistake so many others have lived to regret. Spend some of your time with them. Remember birthdays and their wedding anniversary. Drop them a note or call them just to let them know you are thinking of them.

Respect Is a Two-Way Street

Having said all this about honoring parents, it remains to be admitted that some parents don't get honor and respect from their children because they haven't done for their children what God wanted done. Some parents abuse their children. They don't train their children in what is right. They don't lead them to Christ.

Parental authority over children does not justify tyranny or abuse. Child abusers sometimes defend themselves by saying, "I have the right to punish my child for doing wrong." Beating, burning with cigarettes, tying to beds, or locking in attics is not legitimate punishment. It is *immoral violence!*

Information released from a recent study funded by the National Institute of Mental Health indicates that as many as 6,500,000 children are harmed by their parents or other family members each year. Most of these children are physically battered. Around 700,000 more are deprived of food, clothing, and shelter, and between 60,000 and 100,000 are sexually abused, according to the National Center on Child Abuse and Neglect. An estimated 5,000 children die every year from abuse or neglect.

The Bible teaches that children need discipline. "He who spares the rod hates his son, but he who loves him is diligent to discipline him" (Proverbs 13:24). The sort of discipline spoken of here is administered with patience, tenderness, and love. It can discriminate between a spanking and a beating. Severity of punishment in dealing with children violates the teaching of Paul: "Fathers, do not provoke your children to anger, but bring them up in the discipline and instruction of the Lord" (Ephesians 6:4).

Obedience must be learned, and it is the job of parents to teach it to their children. "Train up a child in the way he should go, and when he is old he will not depart from it" (Proverbs 22:6). To indulge children in their "little" irreverences and disobediences is to teach these traits as a way of life. This matter of rearing children is a place for wisdom, care, and much prayer.

Children need to cooperate with their parents in creating a good home. Parents should not have to fight their children for control of the family. If a child's parents hinder his discipleship, he has not only the right but the obligation to disobey them; under all other circumstances, he must obey them in order to be a disciple of Christ.

Recall Paul's instruction to children: "Children, obey your parents *in the Lord,* for this is right" (Ephesians 6:1). Whenever it occurs in the New Testament, the expression *in the Lord* means "in harmony with the Lord's will" or "within the sphere of the will of the Lord." If the rule they set is not what the child wants to do, appears unreasonable, or is actually unfair, it is still the child's responsibility to obey it. Only when ordered to do something morally wrong or in rebellion against some clear teaching of the Bible is a child ever justified in defying his or her parents.

The primary test of the religion of any young person is the ability of that young man or young woman to relate to his or her parents properly. No daughter can say "I love God" and treat her mother with contempt; no son can say "I love God" and call his earthly father an "old fool" and defy his counsel (cf. 1 John 4:20-21).

Conclusion

Paul said this fifth commandment of the Decalogue was the "first commandment with a promise." In its Old Testament context, the promise appears to have been tied with Israel's future prosperity in its promised land. "Honor your father and your mother, *that your days may be long in the land which the Lord your God gives you.*" In the sixth chapter of Ephesians, Paul seems to attach a much more general promise to this commandment in its Christian context: "'Honor your father and mother' (this is the first commandment with a promise), *'that it may be well with you and that you may live long on the earth.'*"

Most likely Paul is generalizing the promise he remembered from the Decalogue which was appended to the fifth commandment. The Holy Spirit led him to let people of all races, all times

61

in history, and all cultures know that respect for parents is a virtue that enhances both the *quality* and *quantity* of life one can expect on the earth.

The fifth commandment is pivotal to the Decalogue. The first four commandments have to do with our obligation to God (i.e., religion); the last six have to do with our relationships with other human beings (i.e., morality). Neither religion nor morality works when a child is denied a stable home in which he learns to honor his mother and father. We dare not neglect so important a rule in the formation of our values and the living of our lives.

Some Things to Think About:

1. What do you consider the greatest threat to the family at this point in history?

2. What do you know about attitudes toward parents in other cultures?

3. What are some of the responsibilities toward parents and older people which are specifically identified in Scripture?

4. Study Ephesians 6:1-4 in some detail for the mutual obligations of family members.

5. This chapter suggests that children owe a great debt to their parents. Do you think this point is legitimate?

6. Why do some parents fail to get the respect of their children?

7. How do you explain all the violence within families today?

8. How had certain Jewish rabbis voided the force of this commandment with their traditions?

9. What is the "promise" Paul saw attached to the fifth commandment?

10. Why is this command pivotal to the entire Decalogue?

Chapter Seven

"You shall not kill" *(Exodus 20:13).*

Respect Human Life

The sixth commandment was given to guard the sanctity of human life. Life was cheap in many ancient cultures. Unwanted or deformed infants were routinely exposed in Greek and Roman times. The brutal practice of gladiatorial combat to the death is frightening to read about in history books. Tyrannical rulers would have generals, friends, or even family members killed on the spot for the pettiest of offenses. Those were harsh and evil times.

Before we rush to congratulate ourselves on being more civilized, enlightened, and moral than those cultures, reflect for a moment on our own situation. Twenty-three thousand people were murdered in the United States in 1980, and approximately 1,500,000 abortions are performed annually in our country. There is good reason to think we have not come very far in our regard for human life.

Human life is sacred by virtue of the fact that it is in God's own image. On the sixth day of the creative week, God said, "Let us make man in our image, after our likeness" (Genesis 1:27a). We honor God when we respect and preserve his image in one another; we sin against him by treating other human beings with contempt.

Living by the rules calls for a healthy respect for human life.

The Sanctity of Human Life

All life is a divine creation and possession, but human life is supremely so. It bears the stamp of deity. From the standpoint of a *materialist* (i.e., one who holds that physical matter is the only reality and explains all other phenomena as mere functions of matter), it is difficult to think that any value could be assigned human life beyond its chemicals and their price tags. That would place the worth of an average-sized human being at about $6.50. At best the materialist could say that certain individuals have skills or are in positions of unique importance that give them a high functional value. From the standpoint of a *Christian,* however, human life is priceless. Its value is not defined in terms of chemicals or skills but in terms of its origin with and likeness to God.

Because human life is in God's image and thus of infinite intrinsic value, it is a deplorable sin to deprive anyone of his life or even to bring pain to him without just cause.

As Noah stepped out of the ark to become the new head of the human race, the Almighty called his attention to the sacredness of human life and stated the penalty which was to be exacted from anyone who might dare to take a human life without justification. "Whoever sheds the blood of man, by man shall his blood be shed; for God made man in his own image" (Genesis 9:6). Anyone who shows such irreverence toward God as to shed innocent blood must pay with his own life.

The Law of Moses states a number of circumstances in Exodus 21 under which an individual would pay with his own life for violating the sanctity of another's life. Verses 12-14 make a distinction between premeditated murder on the one hand and self-defense or manslaughter on the other; the former offense called for capital punishment, whereas the latter cases did not. Verses 15 and 17, require that a child who strikes or curses either of his parents be put to death. Verse 16 makes kidnapping for slavery punishable by death.

In an early section of his famous Sermon on the Mount, Jesus commented on the Law of Moses and several of its specific provisions (Matthew 5:13-48). When discussing the sixth commandment (Matthew 5:21-26), he reminded the Jews that the commandment was not designed to prohibit only what we have come to refer to as first-degree murder. It was intended as a safeguard to the sanctity of human life in general. Therefore any sort of anger, rage, or malice against another person puts one in jeopardy. Showing contempt for human life in any manner is a violation of the sanctity of life.

The Bible makes it plain that the wrath of God is ever against the murderer. "Their lot shall be in the lake that burns with fire

64

and brimstone, which is the second death" (Revelation 21:8). This is *not* to say that murder is an unpardonable sin. To the contrary, even people who had participated in the murder of the Son of God were offered forgiveness for their awful deed (cf. Acts 2:36-38). But any person who has such callous disregard for human life as to commit murder and not repent of that act will suffer the everlasting wrath of God in hell.

Some Things NOT Prohibited by This Rule

Some have tried to use the sixth commandment as an absolute prohibition of taking human life. In light of the passages already cited from the Bible in this chapter, it is clear that such an interpretation is insupportable.

What is prohibited in this commandment is not all taking of human life but a particular type of life-taking. The Hebrew word translated "kill" in most English translations of the sixth commandment is a very specific one which has to do with malicious and unjustified killing; a more literal translation of Exodus 20:13 is the New International Version's "You shall not murder."

That the commandment in question does not prohibit all life-taking is apparent, for the penalty for violating it has already been shown to be death (cf. Deuteronomy 19:11-13). If the rule in question is an unqualified prohibition of all life-taking, it forbids anyone to execute the penalty for its violation! Such an understanding of the sixth commandment turns Scripture on its head and makes the Old Testament incoherent and self-contradictory. All murder is killing, but not all killing is murder; the Law of Moses condemned all acts of murder (e.g., killing a man in order to steal his money) but did not condemn all acts of killing (e.g., executing the thief-murderer).

The Law of Moses distinguished at least three types of homicide. First, there is *premeditated murder.* This is planning ahead of time, lying in wait, taking the person off guard, and slaying him. It is killing a person in the course of committing some other crime against him, such as the case just posited of killing someone while trying to rob him. This type of criminal act is discussed at Numbers 35:16-21. Second, there is *accidental homicide.* If two men are working together and one unintentionally causes a rock to fall which crushes his partner to death, no act of murder is involved. Numbers 35:22-28 discusses this sort of accidental death and specifies the right of protection an individual would have against anyone who thought his act was a malicious one. He could flee to one of three "cities of refuge" in Israel's territory and claim sanctuary from the city's officials. Third, there is what we call self-defense or *justifiable homicide*. "If a thief is found breaking in, and is struck so that he dies, there shall be no bloodguilt for him" (Exodus 22:2).

Of these three types of homicide, only the first is specified by the sixth commandment. The following, then, are *not* prohibited by this rule for right living or the eternal principle of respect for life underlying it.

Capital punishment is not prohibited. The Old Testament not only permitted but required the death penalty for murder (Genesis 9:6), rape (Deuteronomy 22:5), kidnapping (Exodus 21:16), and several offenses against the theocracy of Yahweh in Israel (Deuteronomy 13:5; 17:2-7).

Moving to the New Testament, one finds that it upholds rather than repudiates the right of the state to enforce the death penalty for certain crimes. Both testaments were written by the same God, a God whose character does not change. He did not evolve from a brutal person in the Old Testament to a loving one in the New Testament. He has always been loving, but his love has never allowed him to ignore *justice.* So the civil circumstances identified in the Old Testament for the taking of life are acknowledged again in the New Testament.

An interesting conversation between Jesus and Pilate is relevant here. When the Lord was on trial for his life before the procurator of Judea, Pilate asked, "Do you not know that I have power to release you, and power to crucify you?" Jesus' answer was not a challenge to the state's right to execute criminals but an acknowledgment of that right; further, there was a reminder to Pilate as to the divine source of the state's authority. He said, "You would have no power over me unless it had been given you from above; therefore he who delivered me to you has the greater sin" (John 19:10-11).

Pilate was reminded that the authority he had over Jesus was not a personal one but only that granted "from above" (i.e., from heaven). God is over all men, and even emperors and his agents can act only as God permits them (cf. Romans 13:1). Pilate would be sinning in using his authority unjustly to condemn an innocent man to death, but those who had used the laws of Rome deviously to bring about his condemnation (i.e., Caiaphas = "the one who delivered me to you") were committing an even "greater sin."

Jesus never challenged the right of a government to take the lives of criminals. All he challenged was whether or not he was in fact guilty of any crime under either Jewish or Roman law that justified his execution.

Almost thirty years later Paul did the same thing when on trial before Festus. He said, "If then I am a wrongdoer, and have committed anything for which I deserve to die, I do not seek to escape death; but if there is nothing in their charges against me, no one can give me up to them. I appeal to Caesar" (Acts 25:11). He did not challenge the death penalty; he only challenged the charges made against him as unfounded.

Around A.D. 56, thus three or four years prior to his appearance before Festus, Paul wrote about the legitimate functions of civil government in the book of Romans. He specifically said that it serves as God's instrument for punishing criminals, punishing even by the use of the sword of death. "He is God's servant for your good. But if you do wrong, be afraid, for he does not bear the sword in vain; he is the servant of God to execute his wrath on the wrongdoer" (Romans 13:4).

Under both old and new covenants, the death penalty is the prerogative of the state (i.e., courts, etc.) and not of the private citizen. Neither Jews nor Christians have been allowed by God to bear personal malice or to "get even" for criminal offenses. No private citizen can take the law into his own hands with the approval of God to become judge, jury, and executioner. God has ordained a legal system within government to handle these matters.

Police action is not prohibited. Exodus 32 relates the sad episode in Israel's history involving the golden calf. When Moses came down from Mt. Sinai and saw what the people had done, he said, "Who is on the Lord's side? Come to me" (Exodus 32:26). In response to his call, the tribe of Levi gathered to him. Moses then gave these instructions: "Thus says the Lord God of Israel, 'Put every man his sword on his side, and go to and fro from gate to gate throughout the camp, and slay every man his brother, and every man his companion and every man his neighbor'" (Exodus 32:27). In effect, he swore in the tribe of Levi as a police force to deal with the outbreak of idolatry in the camp. And that police force was given the right to execute the offenders; about 3,000 men were put to death that day.

Moving now to the New Testament, Peter teaches that Christians are to acknowledge the right of the state, its rulers, and their agents to punish wrongdoers. "Be subject for the Lord's sake to every human institution, whether it be to the emperor as supreme, or to governors as sent by him to punish those who do wrong and to praise those who do right" (1 Peter 2:13-14).

Participation in a justified war is not prohibited. Israel fought both defensive and punitive wars with the blessing of God. Israel was hardly out of Egypt when the Amalekites attacked them at Rephidim. Moses called on Joshua to be the head of an army, to organize troops quickly, and to fight against the Amalekites (Exodus 17:8-16). When the security of the young nation of Israel was jeopardized, it had a right to form an army and seek the blessing of God in fighting with its enemies. Much later in the nation's history, King Saul was told to annihilate the Amalekites for their past history of aggression against Israel and for their depravity of heart against the Lord (1 Samuel 15:1-3). Israel fought such wars not as a necessary evil or in defiance of the will of God; they fought them as the avenging sword of the Almighty.

In the New Testament, soldiers are not required to give up their careers in view of the appearance of the Christ (cf. Luke 3:14; Acts 10). To the contrary, remember that Romans 13 says the state is constituted for the purpose of executing God's vengeance on evildoers.

What is a "justified war"? War is justified when a nation uses its military force to turn back a genuine threat to the security of its people. Just as self-defense is justified for the individual against an attacker or a city's police force against a band of thieves, so may a nation defend itself against international murderers or thieves.

Surely the death penalty, police functions, and military campaigns are things all Christians would like to see eliminated; the ideal situation would be to create a society where the necessity of taking another human life (i.e., execution of criminals) would be eliminated. But in a non-ideal (i.e., sin-filled) society, these functions are necessary.

Supporting such functions is the only proper way to show respect for human life, for they uphold its value in a God-ordained manner. Opposition to the death penalty for murder, for example, stems from a failure to distinguish *innocent* blood from *guilty*. Defending the murderer's right to life treats with contempt the innocent life he took.

Some Violations of Life's Sanctity

Finally, let us identify some of the things in our own society which constitute violations of the sanctity of human life.

First, and most obviously, *murder* is a violation of the eternal principle which underlies the divine rule about life. Our world has an element which has no conscience about cold-blooded murder. Terrorists break into international sports events and waste lives; civilian and military representatives of the United States are vulnerable to kidnapping and assassination in various parts of the world; senseless and brutal murders of elderly people take place in every city in our own nation.

Rehabilitation, deterrence, and the like are not the relevant topics when dealing with such persons; the issue is *justice*. The Jews were forbidden to show pity to anyone who committed deliberate homicide (Deuteronomy 19:13). We dare not become so soft that we make no distinction between villain and victim, that we have as much compassion for the cold-blooded killer as for the innocent person whose life has been taken.

Second, *hatred* of another human being is also an offense against the sanctity of life. Jesus taught that murder originates in a heart filled with hatred (Matthew 15:19). Indeed, the Bible teaches that hatred is wrong of itself.

"You shall not hate your brother in your heart, but you shall reason with your neighbor, lest you bear sin because of him. You shall not take vengeance or bear any grudge against the sons of your own people, but you shall love your neighbor as yourself: I am the Lord" (Deuteronomy 19:17-18). "You have heard that it was said to the men of old, 'You shall not kill; and whoever kills shall be liable to judgment.' But I say to you that every one who is angry with his brother shall be liable to judgment; whoever insults his brother shall be liable to the council, and whoever says, 'You fool!' shall be liable to the hell of fire" (Matthew 5:21-22).

Hatred, strife, and malice are sins against personality. They have no place in the life of one who has committed himself to living by the rules of heaven.

Third, *personal injury* to another person is a violation of life's

69

sanctity. Mugging, rape, or other forms of bodily harm are wrong. So are racism, mockery, or other psychological attacks against others. To set oneself against another human being with the intent of doing injury of any sort is an offense against one's own humanity.

Going a step further, Scripture teaches that we are obligated to lend our assistance to people in trouble. It is one thing not to harm another; it is still another to become involved in trying to help that person with his problem. "Do not withhold good from those to whom it is due, when it is in your power to do it" (Proverbs 3:27; cf. James 4:17).

Fourth, *abortion* is a form of deliberate and unjustified taking of life that our society has come to tolerate and defend. The vast majority of the million and a half abortions performed annually in this country are for the convenience of the mother. The child is simply unwanted or inconvenient.

Of course the fundamental issue with regard to abortion is this: *What is human life?* Some offer to define it in terms of viability, others in terms of heartbeat or brain waves. From a biblical perspective, anyone conceived of human parents is human (cf. Psalm 139:13-15). Or, to say it in scientific terms, any organism with a human genetic code must be regarded as human life. From conception forward, every cell in the body of a developing fetus bears a distinctively human genetic code.

A fetus has the rights and liabilities of personhood, and the unjustified destruction of that developing person is a violation of the divine rule about respect for human life. Abortion is justifiable only in those very rare cases when the pregnancy will bring about the mother's death or is the result of rape. In the former instance, the abortion is an instance of self-defense; since any human being has the right of self-defense when his or her life is threatened by another, the mother would have the right (though even then not the obligation) to protect herself from the jeopardy created by the child in her womb. In the latter case (if such pregnancies ever do occur), one could argue that the woman's will was violated in her impregnation; there would seem to be no moral obligation for her to allow her body to be used against her will for the conception of a child (though, again, it would be a gracious and charitable thing for her to allow the innocent life in her womb to come to term).

Fifth, *suicide* and *euthanasia* (i.e., so-called "mercy killing") are condemned by this rule about the sanctity of human life.

There is certainly no moral obligation to sustain a life by extraordinary means when recovery is no longer a reasonable possibility. The accident victim with a flat EEG or terminal cancer patient need not be kept alive by artificial means indefinitely. But to "put out of his misery" a suffering burn victim or despondent cancer patient is quite something else again. The former is the passive action of *permitting death,* whereas the latter is the taking of positive action which will *cause death.*

Sixth, this commandment also rebukes *the deliberate creation of circumstances which imperil life and limb.* The unprincipled employer who permits his employees to work under unsafe conditions simply does not respect human life as he ought. Neither does the person who supports some "sport" which does not make adequate provision for the safety of participants – modern-day equivalents to ancient gladiatorial combat where people came with hopes of seeing someone's blood spilled. Such practices are barbaric, hateful, and wrong.

Seventh, respect for the sanctity of life also prohibits the sort of *self-inflicted death through harmful habits* which so many of us are fostering. The use of alcohol and tobacco are not consistent with respect for one's life as a gift from God and his body as a temple of the Holy Spirit. And the gluttonous and obese person must ask himself how his lifestyle is really different from that of the smoker or drinker! Any deliberate abuse of our bodies is a reflection of our lack of regard for God's wonderful gift of life to creatures in his own image.

Conclusion

This command, perhaps appearing totally negative to you at first, has tremendous positive impact. It addresses so many contemporary issues for which the believer should be seeking the guidance of God.

It certainly does not follow that this commandment is irrelevant to you because you are not a murderer. All of us have to deal with the problem of keeping our hearts free of hatred and grudges. Prejudice toward people of a different race or national origin is no small thing, either.

71

Is the issue of abortion a contemporary one? What of proposals to end the lives of senile or suffering old people? The Bible says that human life is too sacred to be treated as mere animal existence. Christians must not sit by idly as it is cheapened in our world.

Some Things to Think About:

1. What gives human life its intrinsic worth?

2. Does the sixth commandment forbid all life-taking? What is its correct translation?

3. What is your view of capital punishment? Is it consistent with the interpretation of this commandment found in the Old and New Testaments?

4. Study Romans 13 in detail. What is its relevance to this commandment?

5. How does the Bible distinguish premeditated murder from other forms of homicide? How does this compare to our civil laws?

6. How does this rule for living relate to the spirit of hatred?

7. Is abortion a legitimate concern of Christian ethics? When (if ever) is abortion justified?

8. Is there a legitimate ethical distinction between allowing death (i.e., passive euthanasia) and inducing death (i.e., suicide or active euthanasia) in terminally ill persons?

9. What sports and/or leisure activities come to mind as unjustified threats to human life?

10. Habits such as overeating, smoking, and drinking are mentioned in connection with this commandment. Do you this this is appropriate? Or are these strictly personal choices without ethical significance?

Chapter Eight

"You shall not commit adultery" (Exodus 20:14).

Let Sex Be Sacred

Contrary to the opinion of many people, the Bible is anything but a prudish book when dealing with human sexuality. One whole book of Scripture, the Song of Solomon, is given to magnifying the positive, beautiful, and holy nature of married love. Rabbinic sources even indicate that there was some debate over including this book in the list of canonical writings because of the "erotic" nature of its contents. Many other passages in the Old and New Testaments have things to say about the sacredness of this aspect of human experience.

Sexuality is such a powerful part of human personality and behavior that we would naturally expect the Bible to address the subject. So powerful a part of human nature needs divine direction. We need to know the rules by which this part of life is to be governed.

Scripture has a very balanced approach to matters pertaining to sex. For one thing, it is always tasteful yet very clear in what it says on the subject. That manner of approach will be our standard for this study of the seventh commandment. For another, the Bible avoids the mistake of placing sex in either of the two extreme positions that human thought and conduct usually give it. It steers clear of the puritanical disposition to ignore or deny sexual passion in human beings; it also shuns the materialistic tendency to focus all of life around this one aspect of personality.

Sexuality is treated as an important part of human personality, and sexual acts are ordained of God as a means by which a husband and wife may express their love for and commitment to one another in a language without words. The seventh commandment is intended to exalt and defend the sacredness of sex within marriage and to show us how destructive the same power can be when taken from its proper context and made ugly by sin.

An Ethic of Sexual Purity

There are three basic elements to an ethic of sexuality that is biblical and right.

First, *sex is for marriage* and only for marriage. Sexual contact with a person does not constitute marriage. If two young people are dating and give way to their passions and have sexual intercourse, they have committed fornication; they have not gotten married. That would be too low a view of marriage and too high a view of the power of sex.

Sex does not constitute marriage, nor is it necessary to consummate a marriage. The essence of marriage is *covenanting* between two eligible individuals (cf. Malachi 2:14; Proverbs 2:14). Apart from such a covenant, sex is perverted to an immoral activity; when such a covenant has been entered, two married people share sexual intimacies as a special privilege of their status before God. "Let marriage be held in honor among all, and let the marriage bed be undefiled; for God will judge the immoral and adulterous" (Hebrews 13:4).

There is a special sort of guilt that attaches to adultery, fornication, homosexuality, and other offenses against the sanctity of sex. Paul put it this way: "Shun immorality. Every other sin which a man commits is outside the body; but the immoral man sins against his own body" (1 Corinthians 6:18). In other words, no other sin a human commits involves his person and personality so directly as sexual immorality. Sex is intended of God to be the blending of two bodies and spirits in the most intimate and holy of relationships possible for human beings. Taking this beautiful act outside its proper context (i.e., marriage) is a sin against one's own person, his partner's personality, and the God who intended the act for the unique relationship of marriage.

Human experience bears out Paul's Spirit-guided statement about the particular guiltiness of immorality. Psychiatrists, psychologists, and counselors testify to the fact that people guilty of sexual sin bear an oppressive sense of guilt that is heavier than that borne by most people for most other sins. Surely this is because it is a violation of their very *humanness* before God.

Second, *marriage is to precede sexual union.* Some have made the absurd claim that the Old Testament does indeed forbid extramarital sex but not premarital sex. Their claim is that marriage obligates you to one and only one sexual partner. Until one makes that commitment, however, there is no sin attached to sexual experimentation. Anyone who makes such a claim demonstrates his ignorance of the Word of God.

The one-flesh union of two persons with the approval of God is always contingent upon the prior commitment of marriage. "Therefore a man leaves his father and his mother and cleaves to his wife, and they become one flesh" (Genesis 2:24). The Old Testament makes it clear that a man had the right to expect virginity of the woman he claimed as his bride (Deuteronomy 22:13-21); presumably the woman had the same right to expect virginity of the man she was taking as her husband.

Third, *within marriage the special privilege of sexual intimacy is to be enjoyed without inhibition.* Over the years Bible teachers have communicated the teaching of the Bible to the effect that sex *before marriage* is wrong; we seem not to have done as good a job in teaching that sex *within marriage* is holy and beautiful. Thus people have married with only one view of sex having ever been presented to them (i.e., it is bad and to be avoided), and they did not lose those inhibitions on their wedding night. A lack of balanced and positive teaching about human sexuality within the will of God has created serious adjustment problems for these people.

Here is the positive teaching Paul gave concerning the rights and legitimate expectations of married persons: "The husband should give to his wife her conjugal rights, and likewise the wife to her husband. For the wife does not rule over her own body, but the husband does; likewise the husband does not rule over his own body, but the wife does. Do not refuse one another except perhaps by agreement for a season, that you may devote yourselves to prayer; but then come together again, lest Satan tempt you through lack of self-control" (1 Corinthians 7:3-5).

Within marriage, frequent sexual expression is the norm. Two people must look to each other's needs and see that their emotional and spiritual needs related to sex are being met. Spontaneity and freedom with each other should become a natural and pleasurable part of their relationship.

Things Forbidden By This Commandment

The seventh commandment is stated as a prohibition. It is designed to mark out and forbid to us those things which would pervert and destroy the sacredness of sex.

Infidelity to one's marriage partner is condemned by this commandment. There can be no reasonable doubt that this is the primary thrust of the commandment. Since marriage is a divine arrangement and created with the best interests of his human creatures in mind, God has always guarded it through law.

The penalty for violating one's marital commitment was severe under the Law of Moses. In certain cases, the death penalty was required. "If a man is found lying with the wife of another man, both of them shall die, the man who lay with the woman and the woman; so you shall purge the evil from Israel" (Deuteronomy 22:22). The ancient teachers of the Law interpreted this very strictly and appear to have enforced the death penalty only in those cases where the man and woman were caught in the very act of sexual union. Such people were judged to have no respect for either God or man, as evidenced by their flagrant and high-handed offense against decency. It was this rule and its interpretation which lay behind the statement made to Jesus when the adulterous woman was brought to him: "Teacher, this woman has been caught in the act of adultery" (John 8:4). The evidence was direct, and the case was potentially a capital one.

In cases under the Law of Moses where the evidence was not that of eyewitnesses to adulterous conduct, the death penalty could not be invoked. When adultery had been established through ordeal, a public trial, or confession, the Law permitted the offended party to divorce the adulterer. When a man married a woman and then "found some indecency in her," he was permitted to write her a "bill of divorce" and put her away (Deuteronomy 24:4). The controversy among the Jews about the nature of what counted as an "indecency" became heated over the years. By the time of Christ, opinion had become crystallized around the views of two famous rabbis. Rabbi Hillel had argued that the indecency could be of practically any nature – wrinkling too early, burning her husband's bread, or becoming unpleasant to live with; Rabbi Shammai had insisted that the indecency had to be a breach of sexual fidelity.

Jesus injected himself into the Hillel-Shammai debate when discussing several of the Ten Commandments in his Sermon on the Mount. He came down squarely on the side of Rabbi Shammai: "It was also said, 'Whoever divorces his wife, let him give her a certificate of divorce.' But I say to you that every one who divorces his wife, except on the ground of unchastity, makes her an adulteress; and whoever marries a divorced woman commits adultery" (Matthew 5:31-32). Under the provisions of the Law of Moses, sexual infidelity was the one event which permitted a person to divorce his partner.

The Old Testament prescribed the death penalty for flagrant and flaunted infidelity; it permitted divorce in any other case of infidelity that could be established by good evidence. The penalties were severe so that everyone could understand how serious the sin really is. Have we now come to regard the offense so lightly that extramarital affairs are standard fare for both afternoon TV drama and real life?

The marriage commitment between any two people is intended to be as firm as that which God made with his covenant people. Yahweh loved Israel with an everlasting love (cf. Hosea 2:19-20); Jesus loved the church and gave himself up for her (cf. Ephesians 5:22-33). This sort of unquestionable devotion is the model for all married persons in relation to each other.

Premarital sex is also a violation of heaven's rules for right living. A recent survey released by researchers at Johns Hopkins University reports that nearly half of our nation's 10.3 million girls age fifteen to nineteen have had premarital sex – double the percentage of only ten years ago. Another survey of sexual activity among teen-aged males reports that between 65 and 70 percent of all males between the ages of fifteen and nineteen have had premarital sexual experience.

The old arguments against premarital sex don't have much force anymore. The fear of pregnancy for the girl is minimal. Contraceptives are available to girls without the knowledge or consent of their parents. Carelessness with contraceptives can always be covered by a quick visit to a no-questions-asked abortion clinic. And there is little fear of venereal disease. Powerful antibiotics can clear up most venereal infections pretty quickly. So what do we say to young people? What can convince them to abstain from

77

the number-one game being played in their high schools and colleges?

The most powerful of reasons for refusing premarital sex is given in the Bible. "The body is not meant for immorality, but for the Lord, and the Lord for the body. . . . Do you not know that your bodies are members of Christ? Shall I therefore take the members of Christ and make them members of a prostitute? Never! . . . Do you not know that your body is a temple of the Holy Spirit within you, which you have from God? You are not your own; you were bought with a price. So glorify God in your body" (1 Corinthians 6:13b-20).

If a young lady knows Jesus Christ and is committed to him, that is her best reason for maintaining her virginity. If a young man is a believer, that is his best reason for avoiding fornication. Loving the Lord Jesus Christ means living your life by the standard of righteousness he has given in the Bible.

Not to wait until marriage for sexual experience is to desecrate a holy gift and to incur divine displeasure. It is to create the potential for terrible problems with guilt in a later relationship with a legitimate partner in marriage.

Homosexuality is also forbidden by the seventh commandment. This sin brought the death penalty under the Law of Moses. "If a man lies with a male as with a woman, both of them have committed an abomination; they shall be put to death, their blood is upon them" (Leviticus 20:13; cf. 18:22).

In the first-century Roman world, the church was established in an atmosphere which was very permissive toward homosexuality. Only one emperor of that entire century did not have homosexual lovers; Nero once gave a lavish parade and feast in honor of a teen-aged favorite of his. Writing in this context, Paul identified such behavior as a perversion. He spoke of the condition of the pagan world apart from God and wrote: "For this reason God gave them up to dishonorable passions. Their women exchanged natural relations for unnatural, and the men likewise gave up natural relations with women and were consumed with passion for one another, men committing shameful acts with men and receiving in their own persons the due penalty for their error" (Romans 1:26-27).

Cultural attitudes toward this sin ebb and flow, sometimes approving and sometimes disapproving. The attitude of God remains unchanged!

Psychologists have written extensively about the factors that combine to cause one to have a sexual preference for those of his or her own sex. Help and counseling are available for those struggling with this aberration. But the first thing anyone fighting homosexual tendencies must do is acknowledge that such behavior is sinful, repent of it, and seek the Lord's help in putting it aside.

Autosexual behavior is another type of sinful behavior forbidden by this commandment.

Sex acts are meaningful within God's will in the context of a personal relationship in marriage. They allow the communication of commitment, love, and care between two persons. The self-stimulation of sexual fantasies and feelings through pornography, masturbation, and the like destroys the meaning of sex and reduces it to a hedonistic device.

Sex is not for kicks and tension release. It is for the expression of love for your husband or wife, and that is the only legitimate context for it.

Some Contemporary Ethical Issues

Some of the ethical problems we face relevant to sex are peculiar to our age. The phenomenon of "test-tube babies" was certainly unknown to Moses. This is not to say, however, that the guidelines of Scripture are not relevant to our special situation. The principles of right conduct revealed in the Bible cover all cultures and centuries.

Let us raise some of the issues of importance to our time and see what instruction and guidance the Word of God can offer for them.

What about contraception? Some religious groups forbid the practice of contraception and equate it with abortion and infanticide.

Contraception is certainly not equivalent to abortion. It serves to *prevent* the fertilization of an ovum, whereas abortion is the destruction of an already fertilized egg (i.e., a developing embryo). Preventing the conception of a human life and destroying a human life already begun are ethical worlds apart.

Total opposition to the practice of contraception is based on too narrow an understanding of sex within marriage. It is true that sexual union is the means to procreation of the human race (Genesis 1:28). But it is also true that it serves as a means to marital companionship (Genesis 2:18) and moral purity (1 Corinthians 7:2,9). Since sex has legitimate functions other than procreation, it follows that conception may be prevented by the practice of contraception while the other functions are served. In fact, a number of circumstances seem to call for its practice. People who are not in position to provide for another life ought not bring that life into being. It is often wise for young couples to delay the start of their families until they are adjusted to their own new life together. Then there are such things as the possibility of genetically transmitted diseases which might cause a couple to forego having children.

What of in vitro *fertilization (i.e., test-tube babies)?*

A woman may not be able to have a child because she had polio in her infancy and her fallopian tubes are blocked permanently. A medical procedure is now available which can make it possible for her to have children. The procedure involves uniting the reproductive cells of the woman and her husband in laboratory equipment, awaiting fertilization, and placing the fertilized egg in the mother's own womb for implantation and growth. I am unable to see an ethical problem in such a procedure. It is a wonderful advance in medical technology that will allow otherwise childless couples the joy of having their own child.

The fertilization of multiple eggs, selecting only one for implantation, and destroying the others is quite another matter. That would raise the same issue we face in abortion, i.e., the destruction of developing human life.

What about artificial insemination and surrogate motherhood?

The issue here is different from *in vitro* fertilization – where sperm and egg of the husband and wife are united under laboratory conditions. These procedures introduce a *third party* (i.e., the semen donor or woman whose body is to serve as the host womb for some other couple's child) into the sexual process and thereby violate the one-flesh unity of a husband and wife.

There is a biblical story about a woman who was barren but wanted a child desperately. She suggested the ancient equivalent of "surrogate motherhood" by offering her handmaiden to bear her a child by her husband. This is, of course, the story of Abraham, Sarah, and Hagar (Genesis 16:1-6). You know of the harm which came of such an arrangement.

Conclusion

The permissive attitudes of our day have degraded sex. Sex has become kicks and exploitation and even abuse. It is often a substitute for closeness and a replacement for affection. Thus we live in a world where about half of the girls and maybe seventy percent of the boys have violated their virginity. We live at a time in history when extramarital affairs are so common that the temptation to be involved in such a relationship comes easily and frequently.

Anyone who has defiled this sacred gift can still be forgiven and healed (cf. 1 Corinthians 6:9-11). The grace of God reaches to every sinner, and there is no sin over which a person is penitent that is unpardonable. Unfortunately, even with divine forgiveness, some *scars* may remain and be painful for the rest of a person's life. All the more reason to avoid such sins from the start!

By returning to the sacred view of sex embodied in this commandment, the purpose and beauty of sex are restored.

Some Things to Think About:

1. What approach does the Bible take to the issue of human sexuality?

2. Does sexual contact constitute marriage? What misunderstandings have grown out of such a theory?

3. What purpose(s) is sex designed to serve in marriage?

4. Why is sex outside the marriage context sinful?

5. How severe is the Bible toward persons who violate their marital covenants?

6. Why have many of the old arguments against premarital sex lost their force? What is the most compelling reason for refusing fornication?

7. What does the Bible say about homosexuality? How is this teaching being challenged today?

8. Is contraception morally equivalent to abortion? Defend your answer.

9. What new areas of ethical concern are being created by advances in medical technology? Define your own views on artificial insemination, surrogate motherhood, etc.

10. Are sexual sins worse than stealing or lying? Are they unpardonable sins?

Chapter Nine

"You shall not steal" (Exodus 20:15).

Never Steal

The fundamental principle of biblical ethics is this: "You shall love your neighbor as yourself" (Matthew 22:39). Among the many specific commandments that grow out of this fundamental responsibility, the Bible requires us to show respect for others' lives (i.e., "You shall not kill") and personal purity (i.e., "You shall not commit adultery"). In the eighth commandment, heaven demands *respect for a neighbor's property.*

Stealing is a breach of one's fundamental obligation to love others and treat them as he would want to be treated. It is an encroachment into someone's rights and property. It is taking something under his authority and in his possession away from him, depriving him of something that rightfully belongs to him.

Contrary to the claims of some, Christianity does not envision the abolition of private ownership of property and a communistic society of believers. It is true that Acts 4:32-35 tells how the earliest Christians "had everything in common" and met the needs of certain brothers and sisters by selling possessions and using the proceeds to care for them. But this was no uniform redistribution of wealth; it was a voluntary sharing of goods with poor and needy saints. The first church in Jerusalem had a "daily distribution" of goods for the sake of certain of its members (cf. Acts 6:1). Poor people were cared for out of the church's benevolent fund.

Ananias and Sapphira were members of that first church. They were struck dead for lying to God, not for keeping property (Acts 5:1-10). Read Peter's words of rebuke to Ananias very carefully: "While [your land] remained unsold, did it not remain your own?

And after it was sold, was it not at your disposal? How is it that you have contrived this deed in your heart? You have not lied to men but to God" (Acts 5:4). Peter acknowledged that Ananias was under no obligation to sell his property. After he did choose to sell it, he was still under no obligation to give the proceeds of the sale into the church treasury.

Rather than common ownership of property, the New Testament ideal is work, acquisition, and proper stewardship of material things. "Let the thief no longer steal, but rather let him labor, doing honest work with his hands, so that he may be able to give to those in need" (Ephesians 4:28).

God needs men and women of upright character who realize their earning power is from God and who feel a strong sense of responsibility to use their wealth for heaven's service rather than selfishly. Wealth is not virtue, nor poverty vice; some evil men accumulate fortunes, and some righteous people go bankrupt. If God has prospered you and allowed you to become wealthy, acknowledge everything you have as his gift to you and be unselfish in its use. Realize that God's work in this world can be enlarged by your generosity. On the other hand, if you have not been as fortunate and prosperous as someone else, don't resent that person or compromise your own integrity and honesty in trying to "get a slice of the pie." It is what you have in your heart rather than your hand that shows your worth before God.

Because some hearts are corrupt, greedy, and selfish, there will always be people who try to acquire property dishonestly. Public officials have been known to use their position for personal profit – taking bribes or kickbacks, pocketing funds for nonexistent transactions, putting fictitious names on payrolls and cashing their paychecks, etc. Several studies indicate that many people fail to report some of their income to the Internal Revenue Service or cheat on their tax returns in some other way. Some people lie to get welfare funds or continue cashing Social Security checks of deceased family members.

Stealing is wrong always and for anyone. The eighth commandment is intended to make that clear.

A Biblical Ethic of Property

The Bible teaches us to view the ownership of property as a *stewardship*. Do you recall the Parable of the Talents from Matthew 25:14-30? It tells of a man going away on a trip. In his absence, he committed his property to servants to manage for him. [Note: A "talent" was an amount of silver worth considerably more than a thousand dollars in our currency.] To one he gave five talents of silver, to another two, and to another one. When he returned from the trip, he required a reckoning from each servant. The servants who had been given five and two talents respectively doubled their master's investment; the servant entrusted with one talent brought only the original amount and showed no profit. The two productive servants were rewarded, and the unproductive one was called "wicked and slothful."

The point of the parable is not obscure. Our Master has gone away for a time. In his absence from us, various things have been entrusted to our care. We have different degrees of ability, wealth, education, influence, etc. While the Master is away, we are expected to use those things so as to honor him and promote his interests on earth. When he returns, we will answer to him as stewards.

Under civil law, you may either own property or hold another's goods in trust. Under divine law, everything under your authority is God's property held in trust. You brought nothing into this world with you, and you will carry nothing out. While here, you are God's *steward* of whatever comes your way.

We are going to have these things under our authority for only a short time. It is our responsibility to use them with a view toward eternity. This is why Jesus said: "Do not lay up for yourselves treasures on earth, where moth and rust consume and where thieves break in and steal, but lay up for yourselves treasures in heaven, where neither moth nor rust consumes and where thieves do not break in and steal. For where your treasure is, there will your heart be also" (Matthew 6:19-21).

Paul addressed the subject of how wealth ought to be used and said: "As for the rich in this world, charge them not to be haughty, nor to set their hopes on uncertain riches but on God who richly furnishes us with everything to enjoy. They are to do good, to be rich in good deeds, liberal and generous, thus laying up for themselves a good foundation for the future, so that they may take hold of the life which is life indeed" (1 Timothy 6:17-19).

Christians should use whatever resources we have for the *support of the work of the church*. The Word of God needs to be carried to every soul on planet earth, but it takes huge amounts of money to train evangelists, print literature, buy time on radio and TV, and put people in mission fields. People whose hearts belong to the Lord are willing to support any good work that contributes to the spread of the gospel.

We also use the things God has given us *to support ourselves and our families.* "If any one does not provide for his relatives, and especially for his own family, he has disowned the faith and is worse than an unbeliever" (1 Timothy 5:8).

We use what God has put under our authority *to relieve human suffering.* Because the love of God flows through his people, Christians are possessed of compassion and sympathy for those who are in need. Just as the first church at Jerusalem did, we use the church treasury to care for widows, orphans, and others who are in distress (Acts 6:1). As Paul summarized the matter: "So then, as we have opportunity, let us do good to all men, and especially to those who are of the household of faith" (Galatians 6:10).

It is also God's will that his people use part of their money *to share in the cost of government.* Jesus taught: "Render therefore to Caesar the things that are Caesar's, and to God the things that are God's" (Matthew 22:21). Paul taught the same thing in Romans 13:7.

The temptation is to view our possessions as ends in themselves or as a means only to self-gratification. "There is great gain in godliness with contentment; for we brought nothing into the world, and we cannot take anything out of the world; but if we have food and clothing, with these we shall be content. But those who desire to be rich fall into temptation, into a snare, into many senseless and hurtful desires that plunge men into ruin and destruction" (1 Timothy 6:6-9).

Always wanting more than you have (or more than someone else has) can create the desire to deprive someone else of what he or she has a right to have. It can lead to dishonesty, deception, and stealing.

Think of the Old Testament story of Jacob and Esau. As the firstborn of the two sons of Isaac, Esau was entitled to the birthright. Among other things, this meant that he was due to receive a double portion of the inheritance at his father's death (cf. Deuteronomy 21:16-17). This would have meant two-thirds of the estate for him, and one-third for Jacob. But Jacob took advantage of Esau one day when his brother was hungry and secured a promise of the birthright for himself (Genesis 25:29-34). He later confirmed his position of advantage over his older brother by tricking his blind father (Genesis 27). Greed has been around for a long time.

But surely there has never been a time in history when greed, competition, and selfishness have been so widespread as now. Murder, prostitution, gambling, drug trafficking, broken contracts, lying, and every other imaginable evil can be traced to somebody's uncontrolled desire to get rich. "For the love of money is the root of all evils; it is through this craving that some have wandered away from the faith and pierced their hearts with many pangs" (1 Timothy 6:10).

The *antidote* to lust for money is Christian liberality. The Old Testament required numerous tithes and gifts of worshippers – equaling around one-fourth to one-third of a person's total income, according to some estimates. Christians are not assigned an amount or percentage to give the Lord but are told simply: *be liberal.* As Paul was encouraging the saints at Corinth to share in a collection for some poor brethren, he laid down this principle about giving: "Each one must do as he has made up his mind, not reluctantly or under compulsion, for God loves a cheerful giver" (2 Corinthians 9:7).

How We May Violate This Rule

At least four categories of things come to mind which are violations of the eighth commandment and against which we need to be on our guard.

Taking property or money that is not rightfully one's own. Theft, burglary, embezzlement, fraud, and the like are certainly condemned in the eighth commandment. But so are padded expense accounts and falsified tax returns. It is even a type of stealing to contract debts beyond one's reasonable expectations of being able to pay them or to leave a debt unpaid.

Gambling is certainly motivated by greed for what another has; it is taking from others for selfish purposes. In Isaiah 65:11, the prophet denounced the wicked people of his time who "set a table for Fortune and fill cups of mixed wine for Destiny." We don't know everything that was involved in this activity. It likely had to do with actually worshipping gods of the heathen people around them. It seems also to have involved participation in games of chance, gambling games the pagans of that time were so fond of playing. Several states have legalized different forms of this evil over the past few years (e.g., casinos, horse racing), and pressures will continue to mount in other states and communities over the years to come.

Failing to give full value for money or items of barter. Cheating someone in a business deal, for example, is stealing. It may be in the form of overpricing goods or services; it may be through misrepresenting a product.

In ancient days, people had to be wary of merchants who kept two sets of weights in their paraphernalia. They would buy with the use of a heavy set, and sell with a light one. This greatly increased their margin of profit in selling wheat or some other product. This sort of conduct was specifically condemned among the covenant people of the Lord, for it was a form of dishonesty and stealing (Deuteronomy 25:13-15).

An employer may steal from the people who work for him by refusing to pay fair wages. On the other hand, an employee may steal from the person who hired him by failing to put in a full day of honest labor for him. Either behavior is wrong (cf. James 5:4; Ephesians 6:5-7).

Stealing things less tangible than money or goods. One of the cruelest and most ungodly forms of stealing is to deny other persons their rights in society. A flood of legislation has been passed to allow blacks, women, and other minorities their civil rights in America. To deny education, jobs, or other opportunities to individuals because of skin color or sex is sinful. Many a woman, for example, has had to go to work to support her family when her husband died. If she got a job, she was likely to be paid considerably less than a man doing the same work for the same company. Legislation has not ended all the inequities and discriminations of society. It will take a stronger force than law to alter old patterns in society. It will take the power of love. It is wrong to steal rights and respect from human beings who are in the image of God; it is right to use your influence to challenge injustice wherever you see it.

A student cheating on an exam is doing nothing more nor less than stealing information someone else has and representing it as his own. Copying homework or turning in a paper someone else wrote is dishonest.

Stealing another person's good name through slander and gossip is also a violation of the principle involved in this commandment. Betraying confidences and violating trusts are also forbidden.

Failing to give liberally to the Lord. The book of Malachi lets us know that God regards it as a form of robbery when his people fail to give him the offerings he requires. "Will man rob God? Yet you are robbing me. But you say, 'How are we robbing thee?' In your tithes and offerings" (Malachi 3:8). If this failure was stealing under the old covenant, surely it is no less an offense today.

A Neglected Principle: Restitution

One who has been guilty of violating this commandment must *repent* in order to be free of blame before the Almighty. Repentance certainly involves the cessation of all acts of theft. It also involves *restitution*.

The civil code of the Old Testament makes the obligation of restitution very clear. Several specific offenses and the restitution they required are given in Exodus 22:1-15. And a general rule about restitution is found in Leviticus 6:1-7. The latter text says that one who had committed an offense against the eighth commandment was required to offer a guilt offering to the Lord. Before he could take his offering to the priest, however, he had to restore his neighbor's property (or its replacement value) and a 20 percent restitution. That seems to have been a minimum amount required. In some cases, it was much higher. For example, because of their importance to a man's economic situation in Israel, sheep or oxen stolen from him had to be restored four for one and five for one respectively (Exodus 22:1).

During the personal ministry of Jesus, he had occasion to encounter a man at Jericho named Zacchaeus. He was a tax collector and was despised in the town. At the end of his visit with the Son of Man, he was moved to say, "Behold, Lord, the half of my goods I give to the poor; and if I have defrauded any one of anything, I restore it fourfold" (Luke 19:8). Zacchaeus knew the Law of Moses well enough that he understood dishonesty could be forgiven only when restitution was made for the offense.

Our civil laws today could be made far more just by incorporating this principle. Much overcrowding of prisons could be alleviated by putting those who have committed property offenses not in cells but to work, with a court-ordered obligation to restore and compensate their victims. The largest class of prison inmates consists of those whose offenses were property-related crimes. Instead of spending one to five years behind prison bars, they could be allowed to work, kept under parolee-type supervision, and required to pay a percentage of their earnings into a fund that provides restitution to their victims. Our present system often brutalizes its victims and offers nothing to the person who was harmed originally by the criminal.

Personal relationships should also honor this principle of restitution. Saying "I'm sorry" is a proper point of beginning in cases of gossip, violated trust, or the like. But it does not undo, redress, or compensate the harm that may have been inflicted. People should go back and apologize for their misrepresentation of a matter and set the record straight. They should have the courage to return something that belongs to someone else and compensate for any losses incurred by its rightful owner.

Conclusion

We have not reached the point in history that this commandment is either irrelevant or unnecessary.

Love to our neighbors still requires us to hold sacred their property and their rights. Whenever we violate either, we are guilty of theft. We commit an offense against their persons – and against the God in whose image they are.

Some Things to Think About:
1. Why is stealing wrong?
2. React to the claim that private ownership of property is foreign to the spirit of Christianity.
3. Explain the biblical concept of stewardship. What does it imply about one's attitude toward material things?
4. What is the nature of one's responsibility to use his money in support of the church? What if some of the uses made of that money are not to his liking?
5. What is the nature of one's responsibility to use his money to support the government? What if some of the uses made of that money are not to his liking?

6. What are some of the most effective ways of getting relief to the poor?

7. What is the antidote to greed? How does this work to overcome that evil spirit?

8. Is gambling specifically condemned in the Scripture? Are there any biblical principles that would lead one to oppose it?

9. Show how the following relate to this commandment: cheating on school-work or taxes, gossip, denying others their rights.

10. What is restitution? Does it relate to the topic of this chapter in any significant way?

Chapter Ten

"You shall not bear false witness against your neighbor" (Exodus 20:16).

Never Lie

On April 13, 1981, Janet Cooke of the *Washington Post* was awarded a Pulitzer Prize for her moving account of an eight-year-old boy hooked on heroin given him by his mother's boyfriend. A few days later, the story was exposed as a hoax and fabrication. The Pulitzer was returned, Miss Cooke resigned her position, and the integrity of the journalistic profession was called into question.

Perhaps the saddest thing about such an episode is the way it was greeted by the public. There was a brief, pious outcry, followed by the comment that probably all our news is manipulated, all statistics are shaded, no public figures are credible, etc. According to a study from Cambridge Survey Research, sixty-nine of every one hundred Americans believe our nation's leaders have consistently lied to them over the past ten years. We are becoming altogether cynical about being lied to!

In a culture where truth is regarded so lightly, it is easy for any one of us to minimize his or her deceptions, half-truths, and outright lies. We begin to think, "Look, this is just the way the game is played. If you are going to get ahead, you have to say whatever needs to be said. Everybody does it! And I can't hold my own, much less gain any ground, if I worry too much about honesty."

Lying is *not* a fine art to be practiced discreetly. It is an offense against God and man. One of the things that should be a hallmark of distinction between Christians and non-Christians in our society is the former's high regard for truth. There should be a quality of honesty and integrity about the Christian businessman, the Christian physician, the Christian filing an accident report with an insurance company, or the Christian in casual conversation that sets him or her apart.

One of the important but neglected rules for the people of God to live by requires us to respect the truth. *Don't ever tell a lie.*

Why Truth is So Important

Just mention the word "truth" nowadays and you will likely get something of a Pilate-type response. When Jesus was on trial before Pontius Pilate, he said, "For this I was born, and for this I have come into the world, to bear witness to *the truth*. Every one who is of *the truth* hears my voice" (John 18:37). Pilate reacted – and you can almost see the cynical smile breaking out on his face –by asking, "What is truth?" (John 18:38).

Pilate was a military man turned politician. He had probably gotten where he was by manipulating the truth and lying. He likely trusted no one among his associates and had to stay on guard against their lies and misrepresentations to him. He couldn't believe the man standing before him was seriously concerned about *truth*. He appears to have been suggesting that, since no one has perfect knowledge and human intelligence is not infallible, "truth" is just a nonsense word and has no legitimate place in the human vocabulary. Many people still feel that way.

To Jesus and his disciples, however, truth is an all-important topic. Prior to his appearance in Pilate's praetorium, the Son of God had told people who believed in him, "If you continue in my word, you are truly my disciples, and you will know the truth, and the truth will make you free" (John 8:31-32). He had claimed to be the very personification of truth when he said, "I am the way, and the truth, and the life; no one comes to the Father, but by me" (John 14:6). And just before his betrayal and arrest, he prayed for his disciples and said, "Sanctify them in the truth; thy word is truth" (John 17:17).

The truth question can be discussed under two major headings: (1) factual truth and (2) moral truth.

Factual truth has to do with the accuracy of statements in relation to the state of affairs they purport to identify. A statement is judged true if what is said really does represent the state of affairs to which it refers. The statement "That new car is John's" is a true statement if the car referred to really does belong to John;

otherwise it is false. The statement "Jesus is the Son of God" is true if and only if Jesus really is who he claims to be and false otherwise.

But there is another way to approach the subject of truth, and that is in terms of *moral truth*. This has to do with one's honesty in telling the truth and not withholding what he believes to be the facts of a matter. Someone tells a caller on the phone "Mary isn't here"; Mary is present and looking him in the eye, but he knows Mary doesn't want to talk to the person calling. Or the family and a physician enter into a conspiracy to tell someone in the hospital room "You don't have a malignancy" when the surgery just finished has found cancer in that patient's body; the people have decided, for whatever reason, to hide the truth they know from the person in the bed.

While the two elements of factual truth and moral truth cannot be separated indefinitely, it is the latter which is primary in this ninth commandment. "You shall not bear false witness against your neighbor" does not require you to be omniscient, but it does require you to be honest. It does not demand that you have in your possession the full content of factual truth, but it does require you to be reliable when you speak about some matter where the facts are in your possession.

The issue at stake in the ninth commandment is not so much knowledge as it is veracity, truthfulness, candor, and integrity. Neither God nor man can command "Don't be lacking in information on any subject" or "Don't be perplexed about some difficult matter." But both God and men do have the right to say "Don't tell lies" and "Don't misrepresent something you know so as to deceive me, mislead me, or send me down some blind alley."

The ninth commandment deals with moral truth and honesty. Believers in God must hold *personal integrity* in the highest regard. If asked about a matter he knows but thinks ought not be revealed, a believer can reply, "I'm not at liberty to give out that information," "I received that in confidence and can't divulge it," or "So-and-so is the one handling that matter, and I think you should check with him." He does not mask his knowledge with lies!

Believers must love truth-telling and abhor lying in order to honor our likeness to the Almighty. God is truthful in word and deed (Revelation 15:3; 16:7). Because of his holy nature, God cannot lie (Titus 1:2; cf. Numbers 23:19). The Spirit of God who indwells Christians is himself the Spirit of Truth (John 14:17; 1 John 4:6; 5:6). It has already been pointed out that Jesus is the very personification of truth (John 14:6).

"Therefore, putting away falsehood, let every one speak the truth with his neighbor, for we are members one of another" (Ephesians 4:25). Because humans live in community, it is important that we be able to depend on the information passed from person to person. We must be able to have confidence in each other's integrity. Don't ever destroy your credibility by resorting to lies, half-truths, and deceptions.

To disregard truth and to turn to lies is to concede a foreign parentage. Jesus once told some people, "You are of your father the devil, and your will is to do your father's desires. He was a murderer from the beginning, and has nothing to do with the truth, because there is no truth in him. When he lies, he speaks according to his own nature, for he is a liar and the father of lies" (John 8:44). You just can't deal in lies and be a child of God!

In his enumeration of seven things the Lord hates, Solomon named two which relate directly to speaking untruths. "There are six things which the Lord hates, seven which are an abomination to him: haughty eyes, *a lying tongue,* and hands that shed innocent blood, a heart that devises wicked plans, feet that make haste to run to evil, *a false witness who breathes out lies,* and a man who sows discord among brothers" (Proverbs 6:16-19).

The Bible closes with a stern warning that no one who loves or lives a falsehood can enter heaven. "Outside [the holy city] are the dogs and sorcerers and fornicators and murderers and idolators, *and every one who loves and practices falsehood''* (Revelation 22:15).

Truth is important to us because it partakes of the very nature of our God. In his absolute holiness, everything that comes from him is true, dependable, and reliable. If we are his children, we will have the same high regard for speaking the truth ourselves.

What This Rule is Intended to Prohibit

Perjury. The most obvious application of the ninth commandment in its context is its prohibition of perjury. For one to "bear false witness" is to give false testimony in any sort of civil hearing.

Under the Law of Moses, a stiff penalty was imposed on anyone who perjured himself in a formal hearing. Deuteronomy 19:15-19 makes it plain that the court was to impose on any perjurer the sentence his lie would have brought to the accused person. "If the witness is a false witness and has accused his brother falsely, then you shall do to him as he had meant to do to his brother." If a man bore false testimony in a murder trial and was discovered, he would pay with his own life, for death is the penalty his lie would have brought on an innocent person. If he charged someone with stealing another man's sheep, he would have to restore the stolen property at the rate of four sheep for each one missing, for that penalty would have been imposed on an innocent man if his lie had gone undetected.

Our own formula of this command in the Western world is: "Do you solemnly swear to tell the truth, the whole truth, and nothing but the truth, so help you God?" When one responds "I do" to that oath, he or she is under penalty of perjury if the truth is misrepresented in the testimony given.

While the swearing-in ceremony in a court is solemn, it ought never to be necessary to require a Christian to verify his word with an oath. Christians regard the truth as sacred always – whether under oath in court or having a casual conversation in the back yard. This leads to a second consideration.

All lying. It would be too narrow an application of this rule to relate it only to testimony given in court. In the Old Testament code of personal conduct, a Jew was forbidden ever to lie to his brother: "You shall not steal, nor deal falsely, nor lie to one another" (Leviticus 19:11; cf. Matthew 5:33-37).

To lie is to make a mockery of all human communication and to destroy the basis for trust among human beings.

At this point in our study, perhaps we should be more precise in answering the question "What is a lie?" Is *every untruth* a lie? No, for this would include honest mistakes or inaccurate information passed along unknowingly.

What about *concealment?* We are getting closer to a workable definition now, but still more needs to be done. No person ever tells another everything he knows – not even God. He has revealed many things to us in Scripture, but many more remain his private possession (cf. Deuteronomy 29:29).

Concealment is a lie only when the thing hidden is pertiment to some moral obligation one has to his hearer. For example, Abraham was guilty of lying to Abimelech about Sarah. Because Sarah was beautiful and he feared for his life, Abraham reported that she was his sister. What he said was true, for she and Abraham had the same father. But in telling only that much about their relationship, Abraham concealed the more important fact that she was also his wife. In his concealment, he sinned against Abimelech by setting him up to claim Sarah for his wife. He caused Abimelech to commit a moral offense by virtue of his concealment (Genesis 20:1-18).

On the other hand, there are cases like that involving Samuel and King Saul where concealment is not wrong. Sinful Saul had become defensive of his throne and bitterly jealous of anyone who might represent a threat to his position. When God rejected Saul and told the prophet Samuel to go down to anoint one of the sons of Jesse as the next king, Samuel was worried and asked, "What if Saul finds out what I'm doing?" In effect, the Lord answered, "Samuel, Saul has no business knowing what you're doing. I have rejected him as king over Israel, and whom I select as his successor is my affair alone. Take an animal with you, and, if anyone wants to know where you are going, say that you are going to Bethlehem to offer a sacrifice to me. Don't tell the rest of your mission, for that is between the two of us" (1 Samuel 16:1-5).

Not all concealment, then, is lying. There are some things others have no right or need to know. What you choose to volunteer is your business. But concealment is a form of lying only if that which is hidden or kept from another is something he or she has the right to know for the sake of some moral obligation.

How, then, shall we define a lie? A *lie* is *an intentional deception put into words.* An honest mistake is one thing, but an intentional misrepresentation is something else again. Keeping to yourself what another has no right to know is one thing, but misleading that person with half-truths and silence on critical matters is something else again.

Silence before lies. As surely as this commandment prohibits the telling of lies, surely it also condemns allowing false reports to go unchecked. It is a form of bearing false witness against one's neighbor to allow falsehoods about that neighbor to be told without challenge. It is not only wrong to tell but also to hear (so as to give consent to) a lie.

Discrediting others. It is forbidden to Christians to tear down one another. "Do not speak evil against one another, brethren. He that speaks evil against a brother or judges his brother, speaks evil against the law and judges the law. But if you judge the law, you are not a doer of the law but a judge" (James 4:11). No church or brotherhood can prosper in an unholy atmosphere of malice and fussing (cf. Galatians 5:15).

Are Some Lies Justifiable?

As surely as one commits himself to a policy of total truthfulness, someone will ask about exceptional cases which seem (to some) to justify lying. What about Rahab protecting the spies at Jericho by hiding them and lying to the police about their whereabouts? What of lying to a mad or evil person in order to protect his intended victim today?

What of a doctor who lies to a terminally ill patient in order to buoy his spirits? What of a journalist seeking to find the truth or to uncover an important story? What about government leaders in pursuit of some great goal which will benefit the public? Don't these people in these special situations have the right to lie?

One who holds to the fixed and absolute standard of ethics found in Scripture cannot allow exceptions to the obligation to truthfulness. The fact is that the one in harm's way is more nearly the liar than the intended victim, and our rationalization of lying is usually for convenience rather than some noble motive. Let's look at some of these cases a bit more closely.

Joshua 2:1-7 tells the story of Rahab and the Jewish spies in her city. Read the story closely, and you will discover that she is nowhere commended for her lies. She was saved by grace through faith, in spite of the fact that she was both a prostitute and a liar! Here was a pagan woman who recognized that the God of the Hebrew people was the true God. In spite of her immoral sex life and her willingness to play fast and loose with the truth, God saved her. He did not commend her for either of her past sinful activities.

Suppose you were hiding in my house and a madman were chasing you. He knocks at the door and asks whether or not you are there. What do I do? Some would answer without hesitation, "Of course you have the right to lie in that situation to protect the innocent person." But a few questions come to mind that need to be answered. First, is my temptation to lie in that situation motivated by the desire to protect you or me? The one in harm's way at that moment is more nearly the liar than the intended victim. Second, have we explored all the available options? Who says I would be obligated to open the door to such a person? Bolt the door, call the police, and get the shotgun. Third, if those options are not open to you, there is nothing wrong with telling the person, "Yes, he's here. But I'll not turn him over to you for your wicked purposes!" Might that expose you to harm? Might you have to wrestle with him, try to disarm him, or suffer at his hands? Yes. A brave and honorable reaction to the situation which exposes you to danger is preferable to the cowardly option of telling a lie!

A physician has no right to withhold from his patient the truth about his condition. That patient has the right to make decisions in light of the truth. If those decisions do not relate to health care (e.g., the disease may be too far along to allow successful treatment), they may relate to property disposal, writing a will, or settling some things between himself and his God. The doctor who uses "the benevolent lie" to keep his patient calm may more nearly be protecting himself from the responsibility of having to help him deal with pain and death than the patient.

A journalist loses credibility who will rush into print an unverified report, even if his purpose is a noble and truth-seeking one. James A. Michener commented on the Janet Cooke incident related in the opening lines of this chapter and said: "Miss Cooke's disaster could be titled 'Son of Deep Throat.' In the Watergate case, the *Post* got away with launching a major story without disclosing sources, and a tradition evolved, there and elsewhere, that a reporter did not have to reveal where he got his facts. This was a dangerous precedent, and when Miss Cook refused to tell even her editors the names of her sources, she was free to write whatever she wished" (*U. S. News & World Report,* May 4, 1981, p. 80).

A government whose leaders manipulate people by paternalistic lies is corrupt and will fail for lack of confidence among its citizens.

Truthfulness must never be a mask for cruelty and used to crush or deny hope (cf. Ephesians 4:15); yet hope built on lies is no hope at all. The choice is not between a cold and cruel truth on the one hand and a benevolent lie on the other. There is a third alternative of truth in the context of compassion and caring. Whether dealing with the dying cancer patient or a sinner about his relationship to Christ, it is this third alternative that is righteous.

There is a Bulgarian proverb which says: "You are permitted in time of great danger to walk with the devil until you have crossed the bridge." This seems to be the attitude of too many people about telling the truth. When under great stress, they want to be permitted to "walk with the devil" for just a few steps over some treacherous bridge of human relationships. That just isn't the way a Christian reasons. He wants to walk in company with Christ always, and he will not interrupt that walk by resorting to lies or other devices of the devil.

Conclusion

There is such general cynicism about lying and being lied to that only extraordinary efforts to restore respect for truthfulness can renew trust in the human community. Surely these efforts will have to begin with those of us who claim to believe in God and who give allegiance to Holy Scripture as his will for our lives. We say that we value the truth, that we follow the One who is the Truth, that we subscribe to an ethical system that says "Never lie."

Instead of sitting back and clucking our tongues that so many people lie in so many situations, our obligation (and opportunity) is to be persons of such integrity that our influence will begin to be felt to change things.

The abandonment of an ancient, divine touchstone about the sacredness of truth and truthfulness has brought us to a sorry situation. Only a return to the divine will can avail to rescue us.

Some Things to Think About:

1. Have you ever been outraged to learn that you were the victim of a lie? Relate an incident.

2. Cite some New Testament references indicating the central importance of truth to the followers of Christ. Identify what is referred to in each case.

3. What is factual truth? moral truth?

4. Which of the two types of truth identified in question three is the primary concern of this commandment? How do factual and moral truth relate to each other?

5. Why is truth-telling necessary to be like God?

6. How does the Golden Rule relate to this matter of lying?

7. Is every instance of concealment a lie? When is it a lie to conceal what one knows?

8. Give a succinct and clear definition of your own for the word "lie."

9. Under what circumstance (if any) is it right to lie? Defend your answer.

10. In what circumstances are people most tempted to resort to lying?

Chapter Eleven

"You shall not covet your neighbor's house; you shall not covet your neighbor's wife, or his manservant, or his maidservant, or his ox, or his ass, or anything that is your neighbor's" (Exodus 20:17).

Learn To Be Content

People sometimes make the careless accusation that the Old Testament is concerned only with the *externals* of human behavior, whereas the New Testament goes deeper to deal with *attitudes* and *motivations.* Some represent this as the fundamental difference in the two covenants and the ground of the New Testament's superiority. That sort of condescending attitude toward the Old Testament is wrong.

There is nothing inferior about the ethical norms of the Old Testament. In fact, examine the old and new covenants carefully and you will discover them to be continuous and fully compatible. They have to be alike, for it is the same God of unchanging character who has given both. He did not approve sinful behavior in the days of Moses that he hates today; he did not hate things then that he desires today. The moral commandments of the two covenants are indistinguishable on point after point. The basic difference between the two covenants is their relationship to Jesus Christ. The Old Testament is a promisory covenant, and the New Testament is a completed revelation of the Redeemer.

That the Law of Moses is not content to regulate only the outward person is apparent from the tenth commandment. It makes explicit what is assumed in the previous nine rules about human conduct: *sin really lies in the heart and not in the hands.* What makes people go wrong begins on the inside and only later shows itself in some sinful action.

Outward behavior of a desired type can be produced by a variety of factors. Sometimes we do certain things out of fear; we are

103

afraid of what will happen to us if we do or don't perform certain actions. Someone skilled at hypnosis can get you in a relaxed state and give you suggestions that will affect your behavior later; some people have stopped biting their nails or smoking with the help of hypnotists.

But the best source of good deeds is good desires. The best foundation for a good life is a properly oriented heart, and genuine change in a wicked person's life will have to be produced by altering his state of mind. That is why the Bible talks about "renewing" and "transforming" the hearts of men and women. "Do not be conformed to this world but be transformed by the renewal of your mind, that you may prove what is the will of God, what is good and acceptable and perfect" (Romans 12:2). Both covenants recognize that in order to get to the heart of man's sin problem, we must get to the heart of man.

Breaking this tenth rule for right living can lead to the violation of all nine others. Lee Haines, in his comments on Exodus 20 in the *Wesleyan Bible Commentary,* has summarized it well: "to covet first place is to deify self and set God aside, to covet physical assurances in worship can lead to idolatry, to covet the recognition of others, whatever the cost, can lead to taking God's name in vain, to covet time to advance our own selfish plans can lead to violation of the Sabbath, to covet our parents' freedom can lead to a rejection of their authority, to covet our neighbor's position in society can lead to murder, to covet his wife can lead to adultery, to covet his property can lead to stealing, to covet his good name can lead to our false witness."

It is important for us to be able to identify this dangerous tendency within ourselves and to cultivate a spirit which will hold it in check.

Covetousness: Identifying the Sin

Since "covetousness" is not a routine word in contemporary vocabularies, some of us may not even understand what is forbidden in this commandment. The first order of business, then, is to understand what the term denotes.

The Hebrew word translated *covet* here refers to "enthusiastic desire." The word itself is morally neutral. You can enthusiastically desire a good thing as well as a bad one. You may have an overwhelming desire to serve God, make your wife happy, or provide for your children. There is certainly no vice in desires such as these. Only when our strong desires are misdirected (i.e., toward another's possessions or toward things which would have to be acquired dishonestly) are they evil.

Some case studies may help to clarify what is meant by the prohibition of covetousness in the tenth commandment.

Think of King Ahab and his attitude toward the vineyard of Naboth (1 Kings 21:1-16). A man living in his territory had an excellent vineyard which adjoined some property of the king, and Ahab wanted it for his own. Now wanting to own a piece of good property is not sinful of itself. Go to the owner, offer to buy it, and pay him a fair price or trade him something of adequate value for it. That is a legitimate business transaction and involves no sin. In this case, however, Naboth did not want to sell his land. It was a family inheritance, and he wanted to pass it on to his heirs. If the story had ended right there, no sin on the part of anyone would have been committed.

But Ahab's desire for that piece of land was out of control. He went home, laid on his bed, turned his head to the wall, and pouted. Ahab's awful wife, Jezebel, found out the cause of his dismay and assured him that she could handle the situation. And she did! She had Naboth murdered, and Ahab went and seized possession of his vineyard. Ahab's greed was so all-consuming that he was willing to go far beyond what was normal, right, or moral to do whatever he had to do to possess it.

Take the episode of David and Bathsheba as another case in point (2 Samuel 11:1-4). David saw and was smitten by the beauty of the woman. He had some servants bring her into the palace. Then, even though he found out she was already married to a man named Uriah, he seduced her and persuaded her to commit adultery with him. David's desires were not held in check. He coveted a woman to whom he had no right, and it ended in adultery, murder, and misery.

Another case of coveting in the Old Testament record has to do with Achan and the things he took from Jericho (Joshua 7:16-26). Jericho was the first city taken by Israel upon the nation's entry into Canaan. They did not take it by fighting. It was given to them by Yahweh through a miracle. No spoil was to be taken from the city; it was a "devoted" city to the Lord. But Achan saw some clothes and some money. His desire to have them became so great that he would not restrain himself. Now it is not wrong to wear nice clothes or to build up a bank account by honest means. But Achan's desire got out of hand, and, even though he knew these things were forbidden to any Israelite, he took some of the items he saw. He buried them in his tent and evidently got his family involved in a conspiracy of silence to conceal the act. He brought death upon himself and his entire family. Why did it happen? He coveted.

A statement found in Proverbs 21:26 makes it clear that one can be covetous without ever becoming a thief, adulterer, or murderer. This verse may, in fact, point to the commonest form of covetousness. It says: "All day long the wicked covets, but the righteous gives and does not hold back."

This verse is a rather clear instance of Hebrew parallelism. More specifically, it is a case of antithetical parallelism; the first line names an act, and the next describes its opposite. Notice the contrast in the two lines of this verse. A *wicked man* covets and holds on to everything he has; a *righteous man,* on the other hand, is generous in giving and sharing.

Covetousness is a broad term which embraces all acts of greed, lust, irreverence, and selfishness.

Stated most simply, it is the misdirected energy of a heart set on wrong goals. A person is covetous who lets his values get so warped that he wants all the wrong things to the neglect of all the good things, wants one wrong thing with such a consuming passion that he is willing to sacrifice any and all right things for its sake, or simply becomes selfish with the blessings God has entrusted to him.

Paul helps us get the matter in focus when he writes: "If then you have been raised with Christ, seek the things that are above, where Christ is, seated at the right hand of God. Set your minds on things that are above, not on things that are on earth. For you have died, and your life is hid with Christ in God" (Colossians 3:1-3). A follower of Christ has to put his heart on the spiritual, godly, and good things of life. He has to avoid the temptation to let the desire for things, persons, or events in this world distract and consume him with a spirit of covetousness that will lead him to neglect heavenly things.

It is wonderful to see a person with drive, ambition, and energy directed toward worthy and spiritual goals. The person who doesn't have some great goal in life is to be pitied, for he will never know the thrill of sacrifice for some great end or the sense of accomplishment that comes from having a dream come true. At the same time, it is a terrible waste of human life to see those powers of ambition, drive, and sacrifice misspent on trivial or sinful things.

The New Testament word for this vice is *pleonexia,* i.e., "reaching beyond what is appointed (for a man)." It is appointed for each of us to seek and do the will of God, and the proper use of everything we have on earth is defined in terms of achieving that goal. When we step outside that appointed sphere and let our desires become fixed on the lust of the flesh, the lust of the eyes, and the pride of life, we become guilty of this awful sin of covetousness.

Not once but twice, Paul said that covetousness is a form of idolatry (Ephesians 5:5; Colossians 3:5). It is the worship of self, for it devotes all of one's energies to self-gratification. It is thus the ultimate of idolatries, for it never allows one to get outside the confining world of brutal self-interest.

Why Covetousness is So Hateful

Covetousness is the sin of a world that has turned its back on God.

Only when one has lost sight of the true God can anything else become his idol. This was Paul's point about the pagan world of his time. In Romans 1:18-2:16, he described a world that had rejected the knowledge of God and refused to honor him. It was a world given over to base and immoral passions. And one of the specific sins that had become characteristic of that world was covetousness.

As long as God is in his rightful place in a human life, everything else fits in relation to him. Get God out of the central place in that life, and all values within it become hopelessly fouled-up. God's will becomes burdensome, because something other than God has priority. For the sake of his new idol, a person will blaspheme the true God, break his laws, and trample on his love. A heart filled with a covetous spirit doesn't care about God; it only cares about self. "I know what's right," he says, "but who cares? I want so-and-so, and I'm going to have it. Nobody can stop me!"

It was to this sinful spirit that the very first temptation called the human race. Do you remember Satan's temptation of Eve? It was to eat the forbidden fruit, right? Yes, but *why* eat the fruit? The temptation didn't center on the fruit itself but on Satan's promise that eating it would turn her into a god. He told her: "For God knows that when you eat of it your eyes will be opened, and you will be like God, knowing good and evil" (Genesis 3:5).

The first temptation was to self-enthronement and covetousness. Make yourself into a god, Eve! No reason for you to serve someone else, Eve! Does it sound familiar? It should, for it is the cry of Satan still. Why should you cramp your style by the stuffy old rules of a book that is hundreds of years old? Why should you miss out on all the fun for the sake of some antiquated values that are crystallized in the Ten Commandments? Do your own thing! Make yourself happy! Be a god!

Yes, covetousness is hideous because it involves the renunciation of the true God for the sake of self-deification. It is the most arrogant, ugly, and hateful of sins.

Covetousness causes people to judge all things in life from a single perspective, i.e., worth to self.

Jesus once warned a certain man: "Take heed, and beware of covetousness, for a man's life does not consist in the abundance of his possessions" (Luke 12:15). The point of his warning seems to be a practical one about the outcome of having a covetous heart. He went on to tell a story which identifies the danger of covetousness in terms of what it does to one's values. It brings an individual to the point where his question is no longer "Is it right?", "Will it hurt somebody?", or "Will it advance God's work on earth and bless my neighbor?" The question becomes "Is there anything in it for Number One?", "Will it make me any money?", or "Will it be fun?" Take heed and beware of covetousness! As soon as you get to thinking that all life is about is the amassing of things for your own pleasure, you've lost the purpose of life!

Covetousness lives and breathes in an atmosphere of the single desire to get and never give. It generates the desire to have any and all forbidden things. Even Paul admitted the personal problems caused for him by covetousness. He wrote: "I should not have known what it is to covet if the law had not said, 'You shall not covet.' But sin, finding opportunity in the commandment, wrought

108

in me all kinds of covetousness" (Romans 7:7b-8a).

Once covetousness is aroused in a heart, nothing is off-limits anymore. The law says, "You shall not steal"; the covetous person says, "Who's going to stop me?" The law says, "You shall not commit adultery"; the self-centered person says, "It's my life, and I'll do with it as I please." In effect, Paul says the problem with a covetous heart is that whenever a person possessed of that spirit sees a prohibition, a rule, or a boundary mark, it becomes a challenge for him to defy, break, or cross it.

Covetousness causes one to use his position to exploit other persons.

Peter wrote of greedy men who "will exploit you with false words" (2 Peter 2:3). Once a person has enthroned himself and come to judge everything from the standpoint of personal, selfish pleasure, he will manipulate anyone and everyone in his world for his own advantage. Anyone who stands ready to sacrifice his neighbor to his own ends is infected with the sin of coveting.

Taking advantage in money matters is certainly covetousness at work. Overcharging, cheating, or taking unfair advantage in a trade gives away that ugly spirit of self-seeking. But we would be thinking in too narrow a category if we were to confine covetousness to gold and greenbacks. There are other ways to exploit people which grow from the same root.

Abusing your authority over other people as an employer, foreman, teacher, or even a parent is exploitation. And where do you think racism is fostered? Someone who has deified himself is willing to exploit, take advantage of, and deny rights to other people. Sexism grows in the same soil. All forms of exploitation of other people arise from covetousness, self-deification, and self-worship.

Covetousness allows one to live wastefully.

One of the saddest sins of recent times has been our shameful misuse of the earth's resources. We create shortages because of our hateful greed. It is merely another example of our self-centered, take-without-giving spirit. Whether it is the way we treat our soil or forests or Middle East oil, we want to use and consume without restriction.

Where are our prophets of social justice today? The Old Testament had its Amos and the New Testament its James, but where is such a person in our generation? "Woe to those who lie upon beds of ivory, and stretch themselves upon their couches, and eat lambs from the flock, and calves from the midst of the stall; who sing idle songs to the sound of the harp, and like David invent for themselves instruments of music; who drink wine in bowls, and anoint themselves with the finest oils, but are not grieved over the ruin of Joseph!" (Amos 6:4-6). "You desire and do not have; so you kill. And you covet and cannot obtain; so you fight and wage war. You do not have, because you do not ask. You ask and do not receive, because you ask wrongly, to spend it on your passions" (James 4:2-3).

Preaching the whole counsel of God to this generation of wicked people requires that we address these issues the ancient prophets raised. We cannot afford to get so caught up in the materialism of the time that we cannot see or care about the sexism, racism, extravagance, and waste all about us. We cannot preach such a narrow gospel that its implications for such things cannot be recognized.

How to Restrain Wicked Covetousness

The final, and perhaps most important thing, to be done in this chapter is to identify some practical things we can do to deal with this monster of covetousness. Here are four suggestions:

First, *cultivate your own strengths and abilities.* Rather than resent and envy others their assets, capitalize on your own. A woman sees someone more beautiful and says, "Oh, I wish I could be that woman!" A man sees someone who is wealthy and powerful and says, "I wish I could trade places with him!" I suppose we've all done it in one setting or another. But have you ever stopped to realize that such a wish involves a type of suicide? In order to be someone else, you would have to stop being you! Rather than wish for some self-destructive impossibility, it is wiser to find and develop your own assets.

Someone is looking at you and saying, "I'd giving anything in the world to have what he/she has." Every one of us has more blessings than he or she is using to the fullest. If we would spend more time cultivating them rather than being envious of things we don't have, life would be a lot happier.

Second, *learn to rejoice with others over their good fortune.* The Bible says: "Rejoice with those who rejoice, weep with those who weep" (Romans 12:15).

For most of us, it is easier to do the latter than the former. To see someone really prosperous and happy seems to evoke feelings of "Why couldn't that have been me?" rather than genuine joy on that person's behalf.

It is a mean spirit which resents what comes to others in the form of good fortune and happiness. It is a selfish, greedy, and covetous spirit. It defeats covetousness when you can honestly share another's joy in his or her good fortune.

Third, *trust God*. The selfish, grasping behavior of the world reflects its fear, insecurity, and dread. The Christian need not exhibit such behavior, for he is promised that he will not be forsaken.

"Therefore do not be anxious, saying, 'What shall we eat?' or 'What shall we drink?' or 'What shall we wear?' For the Gentiles seek all these things; and your heavenly Father knows that you need them all. But seek first his kingdom and his righteousness, and all these things shall be yours as well" (Matthew 6:31-33). The person who has no God to take care of him worries that he is not going to get his fair share. But you have a God, and he has promised that you will not be forgotten or overlooked. He will provide for your needs, if you put his kingdom and his righteousness first in everything.

Fourth, *be content with the things you have*. "There is great gain in godliness with contentment; for we brought nothing into the world, and we cannot take anything out of the world; but if we have food and clothing, with these we shall be content" (1 Timothy 6:6-8). It's pretty hard for us to say that, isn't it? We always want more than we have. We are always planning for more things, more expensive things, more glamorous things. An old Spanish proverb has it that a shroud contains no pockets. Are we forgetting that?

When people came to hear John the Baptist preach, he addressed this matter of covetousness versus contentment. "And the multitudes asked him, 'What then shall we do?' And he answered them, 'He who has two coats, let him share with him that has none; and he who has food, let him do likewise.' Tax collectors also came to be baptized, and said to him, 'Teacher, what shall we do?' And he said to them, 'Collect no more than is appointed you.' Soldiers also asked him, 'And we, what shall we do?' And he said to them, 'Rob no one by violence or by false accusation,

111

and be content with your wages'" (Luke 3:10-14). I wonder why we don't teach more on this theme?

The line between godly ambition and carnal discontent is not so ambiguous as we sometimes suggest it is. Each of us must draw that line in his or her own life—and stay on the correct side of it.

Conclusion

Contentment is a unique quality in our time. It is the end result of living by a rule which eliminates longing for things merely for the status, power, or pleasure they provide their possessors.

Contentment will come to us when we escape our slavery to things, when we find our wealth in friendship and our joy in caring about people, and when we realize that our most precious possession is the grace of God through Jesus Christ.

Some Things to Think About:

1. What is the originating point of all sin? Show that both Old and New Testaments acknowledge this fact.

2. What does the word "covet" mean?

3. Show how the biblical stories of (a) Ahab and Naboth's vineyard and (b) David and Bathsheba exemplify covetousness.

4. Explain Proverbs 21:26. How does the verse relate to this rule for living?

5. How can it be correct to equate covetousnsss with idolatry?

6. This chapter says that covetousness is directly related to selfishness. Do you agree?

7. Show that this rule for living would help cure such evils as racism, sexism, and other forms of exploitation if it were observed in our lives.

8. Discuss Romans 12:15 in relation to the topic of this chapter.

9. Why is contentment so hard to attain in our culture?

10. How does discontent reflect a lack of faith in God?

Chapter Twelve

"Beloved, let us love one another; for love is of God, and he who loves is born of God and knows God. He who does not love does not know God; for God is love" (1 John 4:7-8).

One Rule Covers All

The entire Bible develops a single theme: *the redemption of sinful humanity by divine grace.*

The law given through Moses created a covenant community through whom a Redeemer would come and pointed forward to his glorious appearance. That covenant never claimed to be the final word from God. To the contrary, Moses himself said: "The Lord your God will raise up for you a prophet like me from among you, from your brethren – him you shall heed – just as you desired of the Lord your God at Horeb on the day of the assembly, when you said, 'Let me not hear again the voice of the Lord my God, or see this great fire any more, lest I die.' And the Lord said to me, 'They have rightly said all that they have spoken. I will raise up for them a prophet like you from among their brethren; and I will put my words in his mouth, and he shall speak to them all that I command him'" (Deuteronomy 18:15-18).

The New Testament identifies that Holy One and explains the meaning of his work among us. Paul said that the message he preached about Jesus Christ was the one which the Old Testament had anticipated. "Now I would remind you, brethren, in what terms I preached to you the gospel, which you received, in which you stand, by which you are saved, if you hold it fast – unless you believed in vain. For I delivered to you as of first importance what I also received, that Christ died for our sins in accordance with the scriptures, that he was buried, that he was raised on the third day in accordance with the scriptures . . ." (1 Corinthians 15:1-4).

113

The appearance of Jesus, everything involved in his death, burial, and resurrection, and his present reign over his kingdom are the things which had been promised through all the prophets of the old covenant. We are the beneficiaries of the fulfillment of all those promises.

The two covenants, then, are not radically different from each other. The New Testament grows directly out of and continues what was begun in the Old Testament. The New Testament does not repudiate the Old Testament; it brings to completion what was started there.

Marcion was a mid-second-century heretic who held there were two radically different gods and two completely opposite revelations made known in the two testaments. On his view a Creator-God of law, justice, and wrath was revealed in the Old Testament; a Redeemer-God of love, grace, and mercy was revealed through certain New Testament materials (e.g., the Gospel of Luke and some of Paul's letters). Marcion is correctly labeled a "heretic" for his views, for the Bible does not present contrasting deities and discontinuous revelations. Progressive revelation is found in the Bible. The progression is not from error to truth, however, but from partial to complete. It is the same God who authored both testaments and who is revealed in them.

Though we have repudiated Marcion, it appears that many still hold something of his views about the two covenants. Some speak of the Old Testament as that "inferior part" of the Bible, and most seem not to enjoy studying it.

It is a wrong-headed view that sets Old and New Testaments in opposition to each other. Jesus certainly held no such notion, for he said of the old covenant: "Think not that I have come to abolish the law and the prophets; I have come not to abolish them but to fulfil them" (Matthew 5:17). Both covenants are expressions of divine *love;* both state *laws* which teach the practical demands of love.

As we close our series of studies about the Ten Commandments, it is our responsibility to make sure we are clear about the relationship between law and love.

Which Commandment is Most Important?

As we have studied the rules for living found in Exodus 20, have you identified one as most needed by our generation or most important of all? The Jewish rabbis had made a silly game out of such a notion in the time of Jesus.

The teachers of the Law of Moses had identified a total of 613 commandments in that covenant – 248 positive commandments and 365 prohibitions. They proceeded to debate among themselves over "heavy" versus "light" commands, obligatory versus optional ones, and greatest versus least. A professional teacher of the Law tried to draw Jesus into this controversy by asking him, "Teacher, which is the great commandment in the law?" (Matthew 22:34-36).

This attitude toward the Scripture fostered *legalism* as a way of thinking and living among the Jewish people. The "great" commandments were regarded as necessary to salvation; the "least" were regarded as practically irrelevant to righteousness. Salvation became a matter of human discrimination among divine commands and gaining status by performance of the important ones. The end of a process like this has each person setting his own priorities, and the enterprise is reduced to subjectivism. Each makes up his own checklist of important commandments and hangs his hope on his ability to discriminate correctly.

Jesus rebuked "checklist righteousness" and called his people back to the fundamental principles from which divine law had arisen in its totality. And those fundamental principles center on the one word *love*.

The Son of God said, "You shall love the Lord your God with all your heart, and with all your soul, and with all your mind. This is the great and first commandment" (Matthew 22:37-38; cf. Deuteronomy 6:5). The first four commandments of the Decalogue and every duty pertaining to deity grow out of love for God: Put God first in everything! Keep a clear vision of his nature and works! Don't show disrespect to his holy name! Give him priority in the use of your time! These commands simply express in a practical way what it is to love God.

He continued and said, "And a second is like it, You shall love your neighbor as yourself" (Matthew 22:39; cf. Leviticus 19:18). The last six of the Ten Commandments and every element of moral responsibility arise from love for one's fellow men: Honor your parents! Respect human life! Treat sex as a sacred part of human experience! Never steal! Never lie! Don't covet what belongs to another! To observe these rules is to love your neighbor.

Enumerating 613 commandments and splitting hairs to rank them from greatest to least is spiritual silliness. Righteousness is not a checklist of *do's* and *don't's*. It is the practical living out of one's love for God and his neighbor.

Salvation is not by lawkeeping. It is not earned by good deeds. It is not your right by virtue of either charity or chastity.

Eternal life is God's free gift to undeserving sinners. We don't enter it because we've kept more commandments than we've broken. We don't receive it because we judged correctly as to which commandments were most important. When any one of us walks through the pearly gates, it will be because a loving God has swung them wide to let undeserving sinners pass through.

The tension between legalism and love has been real under both covenants, and one extreme has tended to breed the other. A period of hairsplitting legalism tends to give way to a time of antinomianism (i.e., rejection of all law) which, in turn, gives rise to another episode of legalism. Why can't we plant our feet between those two extremes and realize there is no choice to be made between love and law?

Love is the right motivation for keeping divine law, and divine law is the only proper guideline for expressing love correctly.

The New Testament book of Galatians is built around this very issue. No sooner had Paul established the churches of Galatia than some Jewish brethren came in and began trying to bind all the Old Testament rules about circumcision, clean and unclean animals, and the sabbath on those Gentile Christians. In effect they told those babes in Christ that Paul had started them on the road to righteousness and they were going to complete the journey with them. They were going to teach them the 613 commandments, identify the really important ones, and show them how to observe them properly.

These Jewish teachers were exalting rule-keeping and denigrating grace. Paul was stern with these people, when he learned what they were doing. He wrote back to the Galatians and said: "For all who rely on works of the law are under a curse; for it is written, 'Cursed be every one who does not abide by all things written in the book of the law, and do them.' Now it is evident that no man is justified before God by the law; for 'He who through faith is righteous shall live'; but the law does not rest on faith, for 'He who does them shall live by them'" (Galatians 3:10-12). Now you must remember that Paul is not opposing the old covenant here but is opposing a particular view of that covenant. The Law of Moses itself never ignored grace and made righteousness an impossible achievement of human merit. But the false teachers in Galatia had. So Paul continued: "You are severed from Christ, you who would be justified by the law; you have fallen away from grace" (Galatians 5:4).

The same mistake those people made with the Old Testament is made by some today with the New Testament. They identify a number of commandments and leave the impression that acceptability with God depends on one's ability to perform them with rigor and faithfulness. They make their list of rules the all-important test of religion.

Some in the Galatian churches reacted to this sort of impossible emphasis on human achievement by perverting the doctrine of grace. They took the grace of God to mean that Christians had no obligation to any law. They abandoned the rules about divine priorities, chastity, and coveting. They decided to live as they chose and let God's grace cover them! Paul's response? It was equally as severe as the one he made to the legalists. He wrote: "For you were called to freedom, brethren; only do not use your freedom as an opportunity for the flesh, but through love be servants of one another. . . . But I say, walk by the Spirit, and do not gratify the desires of the flesh. For the desires of the flesh are against the Spirit, and the desires of the Spirit are against the flesh . . . I warn you, as I warned you before, that those who do such things shall not inherit the kingdom of God" (Galatians 5:13-24).

There are some who go this route today. They emphasize grace and ignore the moral strictures and spiritual guidelines that the Bible gives to children of God. They are just as wrong as their first-century counterparts.

What is the *solution* to this very real issue? Here is the one Paul gave in the book of Galatians: "For in Christ Jesus neither circumcision nor uncircumcision is of any avail, but faith working through love" (Galatians 5:6). Christians demonstrate our faith by keeping God's rules. But we do it out of gratitude for his grace and not with thoughts of earning or meriting anything from him.

We look to God in faith for victory over sin and its terrible power (cf. Romans 3:22b-28). It is the blood of Christ that takes care of sin, not anything we can do. At the same time, however, we acknowledge that grace makes legitimate claims on our lives. Saved people belong to God and are honor bound to glorify him in our lives. We don't appeal to grace as a pretext for breaking the rules; in gratitude for grace, we submit ourselves to keeping them.

In Romans 5:12-21, Paul explains that the basis for human redemption lies in the person and work of Jesus Christ. He concludes by saying: "Grace abounded all the more, so that, as sin reigned in death, grace also might reign through righteousness to eternal life through Jesus Christ our Lord." Lest anyone should misunderstand the meaning of divine grace, he immediately asks: "What shall we say then? Are we to continue in sin that grace may abound?" (Romans 6:1). Since God's grace is free and abundant, shall we simply set aside the rules and live as we please? "By no means! How can we who died to sin still live in it? Do you not know that all of us who have been baptized into Christ Jesus were baptized into his death? We were buried therefore with him by baptism into death, so that as Christ was raised from the dead by the glory of the Father, we too might walk in newness of life. . . . Let not sin therefore reign in your mortal bodies, to make you obey their passions. Do not yield your members to sin as instruments of wickedness, but yield yourselves to God as men who have been brought from death to life, and your members to God as instruments of righteousness. For sin will have no dominion over you, since you are not under law but under grace" (Romans 6:1-14).

"For by grace you have been saved through faith; and this is not your own doing, it is the gift of God – not because of works, lest any man should boast" (Ephesians 2:8-9). *Grace* is heaven's generous provision of atonement through Jesus Christ; *faith* is our trusting response of surrender to heaven's will for our lives.

In reality, then, one command covers and includes all others. And that command is: *live in love!* If you love God, you will keep his commandments. If you love your neighbor, you will not do him harm but will seek to do him good in every way possible. And the commandments and rules of the Word of God are simply divine guidelines for us to use in demonstrating our love for God and our fellow men.

Law and Love are Compatible

Some modern ethical systems (e.g., Joseph Fletcher's "situation ethics") put love and law in conflict and hold that love may sometimes obligate one to break the rule of an absolute system such as the Ten Commandments. Situations are imagined where love is supposed to prompt – even obligate – a person to steal, lie, or commit adultery.

A biblical ethic calls upon one to recognize that divine commandments are the only safe guidelines for love. We don't know *how* to love unless God tells us in the rules of conduct found in Scripture. Only an omniscient God who knows the end of all things from the beginning could know what is right for us to do under all circumstances. Our limited perspective and piecemeal understanding do not permit us to trust our own judgment in pressure-packed situations.

No one who follows Jesus appeals to love as the basis for breaking rules, for he said, "If you love me, you will keep my commandments" (John 14:15). Again, "If a man loves me, he will keep my word, and my Father will love him, and we will come to him and make our home with him. He who does not love me does not keep my words; and the word which you hear is not mine but the Father's who sent me" (John 14:23-24).

The way to show that you love God is by keeping his commandments. "For this is the love of God," wrote the apostle John, "that we keep his commandments" (1 John 5:3).

The way to love your neighbor is to follow the law's demands about his right treatment. "Owe no one anything, except to love one another; for he who loves his neighbor has fulfilled the law. The commandments, 'You shall not commit adultery, You shall not kill, You shall not steal, You shall not covet,' and any other commandment, are summed up in this sentence, 'You shall love your neighbor as yourself.' Love does no wrong to a neighbor; therefore love is the fulfilling of the law" (Romans 13:8-10).

In the matter of living by the rule of love, we will not improve on the example of Jesus. Listen to his own explanation of the life he lived in the flesh: "I do as the Father has commanded me, *so that the world may know that I love the Father*" (John 14:31). There you have it! Because his love for the Father was perfect, his obedience to the Father's commands was total (cf. John 4:34; 8:29).

The permissiveness of modern theology and ethics is an offense against love rather than a true elaboration of it. If you love God, you will keep his commandments. Whenever any one of us finds himself breaking one of the divine commands, it is because of a lack of love. Love is not an acceptable excuse for sinning; it is what keeps you from sinning.

Purposes Served by Divine Law

Perhaps some people resent and resist the laws of God because they do not understand the purposes for which they were given. If so, a bit of reflection might ease some of that resentment and resistance.

It is God's commandments that make conscience meaningful. That each of us has an obligation to things beyond himself is instinctive to human beings. Conscience is an arrow pointing to God. Because we are made in God's image, we are morally sensitive and know that some things should be judged right and others wrong. Conscience rather uniformly testifies to the rightness or wrongness of certain things in human experience – perhaps murder, stealing, and cowardice have been regarded as wrong in all cultures at all times in history. Paul writes of this phenomenon and speaks of people who do "by nature" certain things that are right because "what the law requires is written on their hearts" (Romans 2:12-16).

But the ability of conscience to lead us very far down the road to holiness is obviously limited. We need more than moral sensitivity. We need specific and practical guidelines for our consciences. The will of God found in Scripture is as universally binding as conscience is felt among human beings. That there is a right and wrong is instinctive, but the clear identification of each is accomplished only with God's help. We need to be *taught* about right and wrong, and that is what divine law is about.

It is God's commandments which show us the style of life that reflects glory to God. The goal of every sincere believer's life is to honor the God who has saved him (cf. 1 Corinthians 10:31). But *how* do we glorify him? How do we know what pleases our God? Scripture reflects divine perfection and illuminates the path that is right for us to travel to his glory.

The rules found in the Bible are never capricious. Human actions are judged right or wrong based on God's own inherent holiness. If an action corresponds with his perfection, it is a good thing; if it goes against the grain of God's intrinsic perfection, it is an evil act. And the only way we could know what things correspond to and which ones violate the divine nature would be for him to tell us. He has done just that in the Ten Commandments and in other places where he has marked right and wrong for us through law. From the prohibitions, we find what the Father, Son, and Holy Spirit hate; from the positive instruction, we learn what they love and desire to see in us.

By obeying divine commandments, we learn to live so as to honor ourselves and our neighbors, thus honoring God for his likeness in the human race.

Divine laws teach us our need for Jesus. This is the ultimate and most important function of every one of the commandments found in Scripture—whether old or new covenant.

Divine law is spiritual, high, and holy. We humans are carnal, weak, and very sinful. As we learn and try to keep the laws of God, we are overwhelmed by our inadequacy. That very sense of inadequacy is our cue to turn to Jesus! Pardon comes from his blood. Power comes from his daily presence in our lives. We cannot be good enough; we can only hope to find a Savior who will take us as sinners, forgive us through his grace, and hold us close to himself in unconquerable love.

The transformed heart sees obedience to God's will as joy rather than burden. While giving his very soul to the way of right living God requires, he knows that God's actions on his behalf – rather than his imperfect actions of obedience – constitute the ground of his hope. The victory is *in Christ,* not in self. A weak and sinful self can only be frustrated in trying to keep every commandment to perfection; even the purest of hearts and strongest of wills is bound to fail too often. We need a Savior!

Paul said it best in Romans 7:21-8:17. Allow me to paraphrase: "I knew the commandments of God and wanted to obey them. My heart fixed itself upon them, and I determined to do right. But other impulses in my being turned me away from that determination too easily. I thought it was hopeless. But then I found Jesus and realized that my hope for eternal life was in him and not in myself! There is no condemnation in him! And now, living in Christ, his Spirit is at work in me and is making it possible for me to keep the commandments better than I ever could before. The Spirit of God is helping me conquer the desires and drives of my baser self and letting me see the beauty of living as a child of

God!"

Yes, it is a beautiful thing which God has wrought in the lives of men and women who have come to eternal life through Christ. It is a testimony to his power made perfect in human weakness. To him be the glory and the praise!

Conclusion

Love is the one command that obligates us to all other aspects of righteousness.

Love and law are not enemies but allies. Never allow anyone to deceive you into thinking that you must choose between them. *Law needs love as its driving force,* or else it degenerates into legalism. *Love needs law as its eyes,* for it is often blind as to how to please or bless its object.

Because God loves us, he has given us the rules which allow for the living of a decent and happy life. *Because we love him,* we pledge ourselves to respect and keep those rules.

Some Things to Think About:

1. What is the relationship between the Old and New Testaments? In what sense is the New Testament a "better covenant" than the Old Testament?

2. What does the term "legalism" mean?

3. Show how the rabbis of Jesus' time had reduced the Old Testament to a legalistic code.

4. With what one word did Jesus summarize the entire Law of Moses?

5. Which of the Ten Commandments are embraced in our obligation to love God? to love our neighbors?

6. On what basis do sinners receive salvation?

7. What is the proper relationship between law and love?

8. Summarize the role of Jesus as (a) Messiah, (b) Lawgiver, (c) Savior, (d) King, and (e) Lord.

9. Discuss Romans 13:8-10 in some detail.

10. How does love keep people from sinning?